Scrapbooking Family

in Historical Events

Scrapbooking Family

in Historical Events

Laura Best

Echo Road Inc.

Salt Lake City

EchoRoad, Inc.

Managing Editor: Laura Elbert
Photography: Kevin Dilley, Klik Photography
Photo Stylist: Jill Hennessey
The one of a kind decorative elements used in
the photography of this book can be purchased
online at www.cgsparks.com

Direct questions or comments to:
  EchoRoad, Inc.
  P.O. Box 900324
  Sandy, UT 84090
  www.EchoRoad.com

Library of Congress Cataloging-in-Publication
Data Available

10 9 8 7 6 5 4 3 2 1

ISBN 0-9770886-1-8

Preface

Genealogy is more involved than writing names and dates on a pedigree chart. Your ancestors worked, dreamed, cried, danced, laughed, raised families, and experienced life in a variety of time periods throughout history. It is interesting to put into perspective where your kindred dead were when certain historical events were happening.

When you research, don't just look for the kings and presidents in your line. Just because your great grandpa was not President of the United States does not mean he was not important. Some of the most valiant people, who worked hard, touched lives, and changed the world for good, are not mentioned in history books but are found in dusty journals and in the memories of grandparents. These stories are worth preserving and celebrating.

Don't embellish your ancestors' stories. Keep things as accurate as possible. The lives of your ancestors were exciting and interesting just how they happened. They risked everything they had to build a new life for themselves and particularly for their children. They played vital roles in building nations and fighting for the freedoms you enjoy today.

Scrapbooking is not only a way to celebrate the lives of your family, but uses a beautiful medium to place your ancestors in context with their environment filled with strife, growth, inventions, war, tragedies, elections, and values. My hope is that something will stir within you a desire to become acquainted with your ancestors. The family members who preceded you have carved you a pathway. The qualities you hold dear are a compilation of those who came before you. The gift of legacy and belonging can heal and strengthen families. Children with a rich sense of heritage are likely to be graced with strong self-esteem, and adults can be guided by the lessons left behind. While discovering and understanding the lives of your ancestors, you will receive a deeper love and appreciation for your heritage, have a better understanding of how you fit into it, and create a precious family heirloom for generations to come. Enjoy!

Laura Best

Table of Contents

Table of Contents

Genealogy Instructions

History is the condensed and generalized summary of the life stories of people. Those persons attaining prominence, traditionally receive more attention in history books. However, everyone in your family has attributed in some way to make you what you are today. Your family's history makes you unique. To find these stories, you will be involved in family and historical research.

Anyone can research his family—no special skills or degrees are needed. Genealogy is based on exacting research, documenting who your ancestors were. Family history is the life stories of the ancestors you find. This culmination includes family traditions, religion, sacrifices, determinations, heartaches, and success stories. These events and experiences are remembered in heirlooms, photographs, diaries, and letters.

Genealogy Tools

Before any storytelling or scrapbooking begins, prepare the three basic genealogy tools.

• A pedigree chart shows ancestry at a glance and helps keep ancestors and relationships organized. Successful genealogy is built on starting with yourself and working backwards—one generation at a time—proving each relationship as you go.

• A family group sheet is used to place each person on the pedigree chart into a family group.

• A research log is used to track the sources reviewed in researching. Whenever you locate a record, write down the source and what information you found—even if you found nothing. This may prevent you from looking at the record again only to be disappointed again. If later you come across conflicting information or someone questions your facts, the research log will substantiate your claim.

Using these three documents you will save time and effort when researching, while keeping you focused on your research goal.

Pedigree Chart

A pedigree chart serves as a master outline of family relations. The chart not only shows how each family member relates to one another, but makes it easy to see what information is lacking. Fill in a pedigree chart as completely as possible before attempting research.

There will, no doubt, be blank spaces on your chart when you begin, and possibly even after years of research. Never assume or guess, as this will later be misconstrued as factual data. Be patient—each blank space represents a mystery for you to solve.

Filling out a pedigree chart

1. The first name (1) is you. Write your surname first in capital letters, then write your given name and middle name followed by any necessary title. (Use the maiden name of a woman not her married name.)

2. List people as couples. Write the male on the top line and the female on the bottom.

3. Record birth, marriage, and death information under each relevant name. Use the European method of dating, with the day first, then the month (spelled out), then the full year.

4. Record place names smallest to largest (i.e. town, county, state, country.)

5. Following the numbers, complete information about your father (number 2) then your mother (number 3) and so forth.

6. Your spouse's family is recorded on a separate pedigree chart, listing you as the spouse.

Pedigree Chart

8
FATHER'S name
Birth date/place
Marriage date/place
Death date/place

4
FATHER'S name
Birth date
Birth place
Marriage date
Marriage place
Death date
Death place

9
MOTHER'S name
Birth date/place
Death date/place

2
FATHER'S name
Birth date
Birth place
Marriage date
Marriage place
Death date
Death place

10
FATHER'S name
Birth date/place
Marriage date/place
Death date/place

5
MOTHER'S name
Birth date
Birth place
Death date
Death place

11
MOTHER'S name
Birth date/place
Death date/place

1
YOUR name
Birth date
Birth place
Marriage date
Marriage place

YOUR spouse

12
FATHER'S name
Birth date/place
Marriage date/place
Death date/place

6
FATHER'S name
Birth date
Birth place
Marriage date
Marriage place
Death date
Death place

13
MOTHER'S name
Birth date/place
Death date/place

3
MOTHER'S name
Birth date
Birth place
Death date
Death place

14
FATHER'S name
Birth date/place
Marriage date/place
Death date/place

7
MOTHER'S name
Birth date
Birth place
Death date
Death place

15
MOTHER'S name
Birth date/place
Death date/place

Family Group Record

While a pedigree chart identifies your ancestry and serves as a culmination of your work, the family group record is a tool used to develop the pedigree chart.

The family group record lists the immediate family of a couple, whether they were married or not, including their children, parents, and any other spouses.

Anytime name spellings or questionable dates arise, such as three children all born on the same day but in different years, underline these notations so that others will know this information may look wrong, yet in fact is correct. This also applies for a child with a name typically different for its gender, or a birth city which is different than that of all the other children.

Do not be confused if more than one child was given the same name. Early practice was to name children after older family members. If a child died young, the given name may have been given to another baby later.

Filling out a family group record
1. Make a family group sheet for every couple listed on your pedigree chart. If someone was remarried, start another family group sheet for that union. Make a family record for a couple with a child, even if they were never married. If a couple had no children, complete a chart and write "no issue" where you would list the first child.

2. Record the children in birth order. Include any children who died at birth or multiple births.

3. Record birth, marriage, and death information under each relevant name, using the European method of dating.

4. Record place names smallest to largest.

5. List documenting sources on the bottom or on the back of the sheet.

Family Group Record

Husband _____ Occupation _____

Born _____ Place _____

Christened _____ Place _____

Married _____ Place _____

Died _____ Place _____

Father _____ Mother _____

Other Wives _____

Wife _____

Born _____ Place _____

Christened _____ Place _____

Died _____ Place _____

Father _____ Mother _____

Other Husbands _____

Children In birth order	Sex	When born When died	Where born Where died	Marriage date/place To whom

Sources

Children's
other marriages

11

Research Log

Ancestor's name

Research goal

Search date	Record/call number	Source description author/title/year/page number	Comments	Results

Research Log

As you work with a variety of records, it soon becomes difficult to recall every record you have searched and the results. A research log is used to record your findings.

As you review documents, list what you were looking for and the results of your search. You may need to return to the same record when looking for different information. If you know "why" you looked at it the first time, you will not overlook the record, assuming you have already reviewed it. If you find nothing in the source, write what you were looking for then record "nothing located" and record the source.

Collecting

Records are created at important events that shape people's lives. The lifestyle and experiences of your ancestors will determine the type of documents they left. The more familiar you are with your ancestors' lives and activities, the easier it will be to find documents relating to them.

Gather any relevant family history items into one location. Check your home for any items such as those listed under "Family records to collect."

Visit libraries to find newspapers of your ancestors' day. Photocopy front pages of newspapers with important dates. Notice the advertisements showing products and prices of the day for things such as food, clothing, household items, and cars to add to your scrapbook.

Old letters from family members should be collected, arranged chronologically, and read for names, dates, and clues to personal and family events and locations. If the envelopes were retained, the return address or postmark can point you toward places where records may exist.

Family records to collect
- Vital certificates
  Baptism
  Birth
  Death
  Marriage/divorce
- Records
  Branding
  Citizenship
  Clubs
  Deeds to property
  Employment
  Funeral
  Health and medical
  Immigration
  Insurance papers
  Military
  Naturalization
  Newspaper clippings
  Obituaries
  Passports

  School
  Social security
  Union fees
  Wills
- Memorabilia
  Baby books
  Calling cards/letterhead
  Journals
  Military/sport uniforms
  Photographs
  Yearbooks
- Family Bible
- Correspondence
  Birth announcements
  Invitations
  Letters
  Marriage announcements
- Heirlooms
  Books with clippings inside
  Jewelry-inscribed with initials

Family Bible

Before state and local governments began keeping vital records, important names and dates were recorded in family Bibles. Inquire if a family Bible or any personal journals of your grandparents exist and where they are located.

If you are fortunate enough to locate the Bible, take a photograph of the book. Note the copyright date to learn the age of the book. Check the first few pages to see if family birth and marriage dates were recorded. Transcribe accurately the information found inside and cite the source as "The Family Bible", the date you saw it, and whose possession it was in at the time.

Check between the Bible pages for newspaper clippings, obituaries, greeting cards, or other treasured papers. Underlined scripture passages or folded mementos may lead to more understanding of the family's values and struggles.

Journals

Journals can be a wealth of information. Some ancestors wrote every day. They wrote about their health and the weather. As monotonous as it may seem, these were important facts at the time. They used their journals to compare the seasons through the years. They documented the best time to plant and harvest certain crops. Also with the limited communications of the day, it may be the only record of events that happened when relatives were traveling, relocating, or at war.

The information found for this layout was found in my great grandfather's family Bible. In his own handwriting he penned: "Iola Elva Death oceared (sic) Jan 22, 1907 at 12:50 o'clock, 4 years, 10 months, 18 days, 12 hours and 20 minutes. God bless My Angel Above."

To locate a journal:

1. Talk with family members and inquire if a journal was kept.

2. Check internet sites by using a search engine and typing in the relative's name.

3. Journals and personal histories may have been compiled in a bound book and available in a genealogy library or with a family member.

4. When a journal is located, get a photocopy if possible. Even one page will show the person's handwriting and his use of the language.

Interviewing

One of your best resources is living family members. Older generations, who were alive during events before you were born, are a wealth of knowledge of family events, relationships, and stories not found anywhere else. Though a personal visit is preferred, if it is not possible conduct a telephone interview.

Continue to interview as many family members as your can. Each will have his own memories and stories. Each will offer a different element that may be overlooked or forgotten by others.

Before interview follow a few preliminary steps:

1. Fill in any family information on your charts that you already know such as your own birth date.

2. Study the people, time period, and event you will be discussing.

3. The interviewee will talk about people and use names in the family from a variety of generations. Know ahead of time who the main relatives are and their relationship to each other.

4. Prepare concise, educated questions that can be answered with ease.

5. When arranging the interview, let the interviewee know what you are interested in so he can also prepare. Ask him to gather old family photos and documents such as passports, citizenship papers, marriage certificates, heirlooms, and maps that you can examine together. These materials may spark a memory or event you may be unaware of and he may not think to mention.

6. Be certain to ask questions about emotions to avoid dry facts. Instead of asking "what day did you marry?", ask "how did you know you wanted to marry Uncle Jack?"
Other leading questions may include:
- What was the happiest moment of your life?
- What are your deepest values?
- Why did your grandpa come to this country as an immigrant?
- Does our family name have a special meaning?
- What was life like when you were 5 years old, 10, 15, 20...?
- What is your favorite family story, superstition, tradition, foods, home remedy, or ritual?

7. Listen and be alert.

8. Be aware of the interviewee's reaction when certain events are mentioned.
- How did he feel?
- How did he react?
- How has it effected him?

9. If you have a question about any documents or memorabilia you have acquired, bring them to the interview and have your relative explain them to you.
- What was the document for?
- Where is the original?
- What is the relationship of the people mentioned in or signing the document? Many times the signatures of the witnesses are those of family members or people with a close connections to the people involved in the document.

10. While you collect information about a relative or his family, write a brief biography that gives the essentials of your ancestor's life. Once you have a comprehensive understanding as to why, how, and when he acted as he did in a historic event, you will have a better idea how to scrapbook the event and capture the emotions.

11. After the interview, you will have a personal account to add to the general facts about the event. This will add life and personality to an historic event.

12. Record in your research log where you received this new information. Name the relative, the date, and the location of the interview.

13. Inquire of family members, associations, and clubs to find out who else may be working on one of your family lines.

What to Believe

Most families have traditions and retold stories which have been passed down from generation to generation. It may relate to a mythical origin of the family, or to the ancestor who lived to a fabulous old age, or to descent from a Signer of the Declaration of Independence. The longer a tale remains unwritten, the greater the opportunity for the addition of errors. And the more famous the person, the more people claim descent from him. Every family story should be scrutinized.

If you have been told you are descended from a famous person, it is tempting to skip generations ahead to see the relationship. However, without a solid base, you risk collecting and working on someone else's ancestral line. Stay focused and commit to documenting your findings along the way.

There are two types of records—original/primary and compiled/secondary. Original records are created at the time of the event by an eyewitness. Compiled records are created after the event by those who were not at the event but have access to accurate information.

Genealogical research is filled with contradictions. That is the reason we look for primary source materials. Secondary sources are used as a substitute when a primary source if not found. Look for multiple secondary sources that are independent of one another in origin to substantiate the facts.

Maintain a healthy skepticism of anything you have not personally examined, traced, and/or verified.

There are impressive websites created by genealogists on the Internet. Some include photographs of family members and digitized images of source documents. While these sites are very impressive, remember that you don't know how accurate the researcher might be. This also applies to exchanges on internet mailing lists and posted on message board sites. Only use this data as clues to trace and verify.

The more research you do on your ancestors, the better you get to know them. As you become more knowledgeable about your family, the more astute you become to their lives, their personalities, and the way they may have thought or made decisions. Therefore, when you do the requisite retracing and verification of the information yourself, you can take what you know to be fact and use this in the analysis of the materials you find. Only then can you determine whether you have data on the correct ancestor or family. It is then that you can place this new information into proper context and expand the big picture creating a more complete understanding of your family history.

Just because this couple is dressed in vintage clothes and next to an antique car does not mean it is 1912. In reality the couple is not married but just friends going to a costume party in 1940.

Cite Sources

The importance of documenting in genealogical research cannot be stressed enough. It is not optional. When you find conflicting facts, you should be able to validate and choose the most accurate source. Question the validity of every source you find. Just because something is in print does not mean it is correct. Write down all pertinent facts until you can prove or disprove them. To avoid confusion, use full names, dates, and places when documenting.

Whether you are working alone, with family members, or with a professional genealogist, it is imperative to know where you have already looked and what you have found to avoid duplicating work.

When citing information from a publication, photocopy the title page of the book or the periodical to avoid copying errors. Also note the copyright information and the name of the depository on the photocopied paper. Refer to the "Information needed for a complete citation" chart at the right to see what relevant information is needed for your citation. Transfer this new information onto your pedigree and family group records. Then file your findings.

Information needed for a complete citation

Book, periodical:
- title & author
- publisher & publication year
- page number

Cemetery record:
- cemetery name and location
- grave location in cemetery

Census record:
- title & year of record
- record location
- page number

Vital record/courthouse record:
- record title
- date retrieved
- location of document

E-mail message:
- author's name (if known)
- author's email address, in angle brackets
- subject line, in quotes
- date of posting
- type of communication, in square brackets
- access date, in parentheses

Land record:
- record title
- type of record
- government agency

Letter:
- sender
- recipient
- content
- date

Military record:
- record title
- file number
- government agency
- location of record

Newspaper:
- name
- date
- place of publication
- page & column number

Online Databases:
- author's name (if known)
- title of article, in quotation marks
- the series name (if applicable)
- date of publication
- name of database (if applicable)
- name of the online service
- directory path followed
- date accessed, in parentheses

Oral interview:
- interviewee's name
- interviewer's name
- date of interview

Photograph:
- date photograph was taken
- identification of people

Telephone conversation:
- date
- interviewee's name
- phone number & address

WWW site:
- author's name (if known)
- document title, in quotes
- publication date
- WWW address (URL), in angle brackets
- access date, in parenthesis

Photography

Photographs are extremely important in research, not only to visualize your ancestors but to see the details in the photographs. Photographs need not have people in them—pictures of old family houses, automobiles, and businesses will add to the historical interest of a family. They will also give some personal information and perspective on the time period and living conditions of the family.

Photographs were not a high priority to your ancestors, or may not have been available, the further back in history you go. You may be fortunate and have a number of family photographs, however, most people will find that their heritage photographs are limited. Don't be discouraged. Cherish the ones you are able to locate.

Photos may be found in old photo albums and scrapbooks. Most likely these were made of acidic, unstable materials. The adhesives will eventually discolor, become brittle, and damage the photos. Carefully remove images from old scrapbooks.

Don't overlook slides and reel-to-reel 8mm films. Photographs can be made from these mediums at a relatively low cost through your local photo store.

Photograph & film care

1. Keep photographs and film away from dirt, dust, and the natural oil on your hands. To handle an image use latex or cotton gloves.

2. Remove photographs from harmful existing environments such as magnetic albums. Such albums are typically highly acidic and dangerous to photos.

3. Do not write on the front or back of a photograph with a ballpoint or felt-tipped pen, the acid in ink will deteriorate or stain photographs.

4. Do not display important original photographs. Over time the glass may stick to the emulsion while sunlight will cause the photos to fade. If you want to display a precious photograph, have a copy made and display the copy.

5. Do not use glues or tapes to mend photographs. Most glues contain substances which will cause photos to deteriorate.

Photograph Removal

Older family photographs may have been stored and preserved in black paper scrapbooks or photo albums with a magnetic surface to hold photos in place under plastic. Both of these types of albums have been found to be detrimental to photographs over time due to their high acid content. To preserve the photographs currently in these situations, remove the photographs and paper documents stored in this manner.

If glue was used to hold down the photographs, carefully try to lift the photos off of the album page with a small spatula to see if you can remove them easily. Slip the spatula under the edge of the photo, and carefully move it back and forth. The ease with which the photos come up varies depending on the humidity level. Dry conditions may make prints and backing brittle, easier to lift. Humid conditions may soften the adhesive and ease removal. Do not force the photos so that they tear.

If you cannot lift them, cut away the black paper around the photo. If there are photos are on both sides of the page and you cannot cut around, interweave the pages of the album with acid-free paper and store the album in an acid-free box.

The photographs in a magnetic scrapbook should come off quite easily once you lift the plastic sheet which holds them in place. If a photograph was additionally glued in place, or the photo has "melted" to the page, slip a small spatula under each photo to pry from the page.

Photo Identification

Family photographs contribute a large amount of historical information and detail. When dating an image, remember it takes several pieces of information to assign a date, and one definite piece of data is not enough. This becomes essential when working with an image that is a copy of an earlier photograph or a picture in which the costume clues imply one timeframe but the genealogical information suggests another. It is the sum total of the details that decide on a date. Follow a few different steps to determine the date of a photograph. Refer to the Photo identification steps below to determine the date of your mystery photographs.

Photo identification steps

1. Ask older family members to identify people, dates, and events.

2. Take photos out of frames. Some frames held numerous photographs stacked on top of one another. Compare these photos to one another. Most likely they are of the same family.

3. Look for distinct items in the photograph for a date. For instance, a calendar or newspaper present in the image can assign a month and year to the scene. Another apparent clue is a handwritten note on the back of the image with a year. However, don't rely completely on this information, as it could have been erroneously written on the back by later relatives who thought they knew the date.

4. If the photographer's name, address, or studio name and address are stamped on the photograph contact the studio.

5. Look at the internal details in the photograph. Are there cars, sports equipment, or signs present? If so, research the types of items people used during that time period.

6. Occupational photographs can often put a date to uniforms, badges, and equipment present in the images.

7. Photos can be dated by the developing process. Refer to Photo Identification through Processing on pages 21–23.

8. The time period may be determined by the clothing worn in the photograph. Refer to the Photo Identification Through Women's and Men's Fashion on pages 24–29.

Photo Identification through Processing

1839–1860 The daguerreotype uses a polished, silver plated sheet of metal, and once seen is easily recognized by its mirror-like surface. The plate must be held at the correct angle to the light for the image to be visible. The image is extremely sharp and detailed. It was common to place a daguerreotype in oval silver frames or apply to jewelry such as watches or brooches.

Both the California Gold Rush and the Westward expansion were among the first major historical events to be captured by the daguerreotypists camera.

Some portraits had a small amount of coloring added by artificial means. Usually this coloring was limited to the cheeks and jewelry, but on occasion the complete image was colored.

1854–1865 The ambrotype is a positive photographic image on glass. The image resembled a negative, but would appear positive when the plate was given a coat of varnish backing on the reverse side. A completed ambrotype was normally placed in a case of wooden or plastic design.

Negative glass plate

Positive glass plate

1856–1867 The tintype is a negative image produced on a thin metal plate. The image is viewed as positive due to undercoating of black varnish.

Tintypes can be the hardest pictures to assign a date to because of their long run of popularity, and the lack of photographer's imprint and other clues. Most tintypes from the 1860s have black backs, while those produced after 1870 are generally brown. Other than that, you mostly have to rely on clothing styles to determine the date.

The easiest way to differentiate an ambrotype and a tintype is to remove the image from its case and look at the back. If the image is of glass, then it is an ambrotype. If it is of black, gray, or brown-coated metal, it is a tintype.

Daguerreotype

Ambrotype

Tintype

1863–1900 The cabinet card is easily distinguished from other card mounted photos by its size, typically 4.25" x 6.5". The majority are portraits, and most of them are not identified with the subjects name. Many have a photographers imprint. Photographic paper was very thin in the 1800s, so paper prints were pasted to cardboard mounts. Card mounted photographs offer a wide variety of clues about their date.

The photographer's imprint is a clue to the date of the photograph. Not only can you use external sources like directories and local histories to determine what years that photographer was in business at the location listed, but the imprint itself has stylistic features that changed over the years. As a general rule, simple imprints were used at first, then they gradually became more ornate, until about 1885, when there was a divergence, with some photographers going back to simpler imprints, while others continued to use more ornate styles. On the backs of cards, the styles changed through the years. If the imprint is small and plain, then a single line imprint usually dates from 1860-62. Two or four lines from 1861-66. If these two to four line imprints have the statements "Duplicates can be had" or "negatives preserved" they date from 1863 or later. Four or more lines with larger type characters and often additional information date from 1863-67. Imprints with curved lines of text with curved lines and curlicues between and around them date from 1863-65. After 1867, most imprints became larger.

From 1862 to 1865 it was popular to have a frame around the imprint, with various geometric patterns and lines. A logo above the imprint, such as an eagle, artist's palette, Liberty, etc., was used from 1862 to 1866. The cherub and camera logo was in style from 1865 to 1872. The logo of a photographic association, the NPA, was used from 1871 to 1874. After 1872 the photographer's imprint was often a large, elaborate design that covered most of the back of the card. Those using an Egyptian or oriental motif usually date from 1881 to 1886.

The presence of a tax stamp on the back of a photograph indicates that it was taken during the Civil War by a photographer on the Union side, and dates between 1864 –1866.

The image itself may also hold clues as to the date. If the image is of the head only, or head and shoulders, the size of the head can be an indication of the date. If the head is ¾" wide, or less, it usually dates from 1860 to 1864. If it is about 1" wide, then it likely dated from 1860 to 1867. If it is 1¼"–1¾", then it dates from 1866 to 1875.

1850–1890 Albumen prints were produced from a glass negative on paper coated with egg whites. Because the paper was so thin, the drying emulsion tended to cause the paper to curl, hence the practice of pasting the papers to cardboard. Though the surface is glossy the procedure cannot produce true black or white tones. There is a red-brown or purple image tone and some cracking and yellowing.

Cabinet card

Albumen print

1854–1900 *Carte de visite* (CDV's) are a type of card mounted photograph. The CDV is easily distinguished from other card mounted photos by its size, typically 2½" x 4". The various characteristics of card mount, image and photographer's imprint often allows these images to be correctly dated to within a few years of their origin.

During the early 1860s, Americans learned the ability to capture and hold a memory. The carte de visite portrayed sons and fathers gone to war, wives and children left behind, and heroes both alive and fallen. Photography was so popular during the Civil War that a special revenue bill was passed requiring an additional tax stamp to be affixed to any photographs sent through the mail.

1854 to 1938 *Stereographs* are normally mounted on cardboard and are easily recognized by having two nearly identical images mounted side by side. When looked at through a stereoscope, they give a three-dimensional image.

Stereograph were produced solely for entertainment and informational purposes. The shots may be identical or have some variance. They were made either by moving the camera to produce two plates exposed from different angles or by taking two separate exposures on two cameras sitting side by side.

1910-1925 *Postcards* were developed in studios to produce portraits on postcards, rather than the slightly larger, more substantial Cabinet Prints that had been mounted on thick card in earlier years. The common picture postcard can be a source of historical documentation.

In this period, cameras were sold that took a postcard-sized image,

Postcard

and photographers provided prints on postcard stock, so there are many personal snapshot images from that period. Mass produced postcards were often photomechanical prints, usually lithographs.

Carte-de-visite

Stereograph

Photo Identification Through Women's Fashions

When determining a time period looking at the style of clothing, hair and general dress may give some clues as to the era. Do not assume. If you see a photo the subjects could purposely be dressing from the past such as girls dressing for a 50s party in the 90s. However it is safe to say the photographs are not going to be older than you think. They are not going to have a telephone in a photograph before they were invented. Since photographs in the 19th century were not the impromptu snapshots of today, but formal occasions that required one's best dress we will discuss woman's attire in her best wear to determine the era.

1840-1850

Women's fashions consisted of floor length dresses with bell-shaped skirts over many layers of thick petticoats, and very constrictive corset, giving a flattened and upward spreading bustline. Sleeves tended to be narrow, the bodice long and tight, and almost always closing in the back. Collars were always white, of varying styles. Bonnets were popular, with deep, face concealing brim, and long drooping ends. An elbow-length cape called a pelerine was often worn. Hair was parted in the middle and drawn back, over the ears. Younger women might have dangling curls.

1850-1854

Lace cap threaded with wide black ribbon. In order to make the skirt appear more full, women were wearing a petticoat. Early ones were made of horsehair and later they were made with stiff wire or whalebone to enlarge the "hoop" skirt.

Short corsets became the dominant fashion. Introducing the plain, one-piece dress style with a moderately long waist and bishop's sleeves, opening at the front of the bodice. Necklines were more open than before, and wider collars were in style. Collars as wide as 3"–3½" were worn flat on the shoulders, rather than upright as had been the earlier style.

1855–1859

The hooped skirt was replacing voluminous petticoats. The sleeves were full and gathered or narrowed at the wrist. Hair was parted in the center and pulled back with ears exposed. Elegant hats had low-crowned and were trimmed with feathers.

1860–1864

Dresses had wide and billowing sleeves in bell shaped flares or more modestly flaring bishop's sleeves. Bolero-type jackets were fashionable.

The Civil War caused some disruption of fashion trends, particularly in the South. Cloth of any kind was at a premium, and much effort went into providing the soldiers with warm clothes and blankets.

1840-1850

1850-1854

1855-1859

1860-1864

Women wore bodices that buttoned down the front with a round or pointed waist decorated with military trim. Necklines featured high, round collars, while some had V-necks with lapels. Armholes were over the shoulder, with sleeves gathering into the wrist or wide bells in a variety of styled. Skirts worn over a hoop were fully pleated and adorned with applied geometric decorations and wide belts.

Accessories included shawls, hairnets, elaborate earrings, and broaches. Hair was worn with a center part and either pulled straight back or high on the head.

1865–1874

Bodices fastened down the front, usually with buttons, and generally had two darts on either side of the front. Small collars were again in fashion, and many dress styles were tight to the base of the neck. Dresses became narrow when viewed from the front, but often had a bustle or bulge at the back. Corsets were short. The waistline was high. There was much use of pleating and ruffled flounces. Black velvet neck ribbons were worn tied at back with a bow, with a brooch at the front. Bodices featured trim such as ruffles and prominent buttons. Necklines were high with low standing collar.

1875–1877

Ruffles were seen around the neckline and down the front, with a front opening neckline featuring a low standing collar or V-neck with ruffles. Sleeves were narrow with trim. Skirts had long overskirt effects, bustles were small and trains were common. Waistlines began to lengthen. A simple, single drop earring became fashionable, as hair was drawn close at the sides of the head.

False hair was popular with large hair combs; some hair curled at the forehead; long hair could be worn streaming down the back with hair braided at the crown. Fancy hats were common riding high on the head and dropping in the back.

1878–1882

Bodices featured front buttons with the bodice extending over the hips. Necklines were high with low standing collars. Sleeves remained narrow and skirts fell straight from hip to floor. Fans and parasols were common. Hair was worn with a center part with some frizzing, and buns appeared low at the back.

1883–1890

The bustle returned, with side pads that widened the hips. Skirts became fuller with some padding at the back. Tight bodices with waistcoat effects extended below the waist. High necklines had low standing collars and fewer lace ties. Sleeves were tight, ¾ lengths, with trim at the bottom. By 1887, the bustle shape was deflated, forming drooping, deep folds. At the end of the decade a new, narrow skirt style was adopted, with fullness in the back. Bodices were worn tight, with high collars. Sleeves were mostly narrow, and ended tight at the wrist.

1865-1874

1875-1877

1878-1882

1883-1890

1891–1895

Skirts remained full with some train. Sleeves became narrower with a small vertical puff at the shoulder, which over the next few years expanded into the full "leg-o-mutton" sleeve. The collar was of starched white fabric and adorned with a cameo or brooch. The sleeve cuffs normally match the collar with a wider lace covering part of the hand.

Another popular outfit was a blouse called a shirtwaist, which was worn with a separate skirt. At this time, the "hourglass" figure became popular and the woman's clothing was laced tight at the waist to make the waist as small as possible. Hair combs were still popular with ringlets or false hair.

1896–1900

Bodices were symmetrical with horizontal drapery and blouse-like fullness over the waist. Sleeves became smaller, with fullness at the top and tight flaring over the hand. Women wore small earrings, a watch pinned to the bosom of their dress, and small decorative combs high on the back of the head that were visible from the front. Hair was worn frizzed around the face with a back bun. Hats were still in style yet had become smaller.

1901–1910

Slim skirts that flared out below the knees, with bodices featuring tight sleeves that flared over the hand. Their accessories included round brooches, watches, small earrings, and combs to hold their hair back in a bun. Pouched front bodices featured a wide waistband. Collars were high to the chin. Sleeve fullness increased by the year on the lower arms, and cuffs were seen by mid-decade. Women wore their hair in a soft back bun that became fuller later in the decade. Styles changed quickly as manufacturers made clothing and a mass market developed.

1911–1914

Vertical trim was popular on dresses as were small square dickeys with raised waistlines. Collars varied from high to the chin and round, or square to the collarbone. Sleeves increased in tightness in this period. Skirts are slim and straight, revealing the shoes. Hair was full and puffed out at the side, to be worn with large hats.

The style called a hobble skirt was in fashion with the skirt so tight at the bottom that women had trouble walking. Clothing became looser, lightweight, and less formal.

1915–1919

During World War I, simple styles prevailed. The hobble skirt had been replaced by full skirts with a belted overdress. Hairstyles were simple and brushed low over the forehead and ears. Working women found short hair more manageable and hair between the earlobe and the shoulder became popular. Dresses were made of softer, thinner fabrics which breathed easier and were easier to launder. Due to the war, the changing of style slowed and became more and more simple and understated.

1891–1895 1896–1900 1901–1910 1911–1914 1915–1919

1920–1925

Dresses became a straight design, unfitted, with skirts about knee length. The term "flapper" was the word that characterizes this time, which in the dictionary means dress that has somewhat daring freedom and boldness.

The more conservative women, living in the country, wore a looser fitting dress with a lowered waist. Dresses were mid-calve length showing more leg than in the past. Long necklaces and brooches were common as well as ribbons.

1926–1929

Dresses remained ankle length and slimming. Multiple ruffles were popular around the thigh and the neckline. Dresses were accessorized with thin belts, long chains, and thin jackets.

Hair styles became short and curly and were adorned with head bands, ribbons, and combs. Dresses were manufactured in bulk and outfits were less unique from one another as in past years.

1930–1940

Women began wearing slacks and skirt styles were longer. Motion pictures that were now coming out in color were a popularity of this time influencing fashion. People looked to escape the reality of poverty by imitating the glamour fashion of movie stars.

The style was the natural form of the body. Zippers were introduced and many wore clingy styles. Fur capes, coats, stoles, wraps, and trimmings were a popular accessory. A popular length for this time is to wear calf-length by day and full length for night. Hats were essential accessories during wintertime, although it had again became popular to adorn them with decoration, such as a hatpin or a decorative finish to the hat itself. It was customary during this period to wear hats tilted to the side. Pearl necklaces were especially sought after.

Women saw cosmetics as an inexpensive means of altering their appearance and boosting their self-esteem. Women were accepted in pants.

1941–1950

Skirts were shorter, and blouse and skirts were the fitted design. Padded shoulders were also common in blouses and jacket styles.

After World War II, long full skirts were again popular with nylon and other materials for shorter hemline and straight fitting sheath dresses, but we also think of the poodle skirts in this time frame which were in fashion. Also the A line dress and shift dresses, and the mini-skirt came into fashion.

Depending on the livelihood and where they lived, slacks were commonly worn. Women living and working in the fields of the West were often seen in pants and cotton pull over shirts. In an effort to protect the face and keep a white skin tone, it was common to wear a wide-brimmed hat in the field when gardening.

Though men were wearing jeans, women's pants were still of heavy cotton fabric.

Hairstyles in the West remained short, while in the East they began to grow longer.

1920–1925   **1926–1929**   **1930–1940**   **1941–1950**

Photo Identification Through Men's Fashions

Men's fashions are not as telling as women's. However, there were time periods when clothing was quite distinctive to the time period. A gentleman's attire was to be subtle and not attract attention unless it be for neatness and propriety.

Farmers, laborers, ranchers, and factory workers usually wore an outfit of sturdy wool, corduroy, or denim trousers, a wool flannel, linen or cotton pull over shirt, a hat and sturdy shoes. Suspenders were commonly worn, though they were unpopular with men who had to bend or squat a lot, like sailors, cowboys, or miners.

1830–1840

Everyday clothing consisted of a linen pullover shirt, made with full sleeves, deep buttoned cuffs, a generous collar, and very long tails to tuck into the trousers. Underwear was not worn, so the tails helped protect the wearer from the scratchy wool of the trousers. The pants had straight, fairly slim legs, and a flap which buttoned to the waistband in front covered pockets on either side of the opening. A cravat, covered the throat. A vest was always worn, either single or double breasted, with or without a collar, whether or not a coat went over it. It helped to hide the suspenders, or galluses, which held up the trousers.

1840-1850

Frock coats with M-notch lapels were popular with a matching waistcoat, and a cravat tied in a simple knot. Coats were fitted at the waist with short flaring skirts. The double-breasted frock coat had silk-faced lapels and closed skirt front. Pockets were placed in the back of the skirt and usually the coat had a luxurious velvet collar.

Heavy tweed suits came into use for sportswear, and the dinner coat without tails was used for dinners and dances in country homes.

Pants were cotton or wool with mule ear pockets and reinforced riding area.

1851-1860

Wide-brimmed, flat-crowned hats were worn at a tilt. Partial beard and mustache were common. Wide bow ties were worn with fringe at one end. Plaid waistcoat and coat were popular with tab fastening.

An outfit consisted of three distinct colors: one for the jacket, one for the waistcoat and a third for the trousers.

Braid trimmings along with the customary laces were found on men's clothes. It was used as decorative trim on coats and stitched down the side seams of trousers and survives today on the trousers of the tail and dinner coats. Both trousers and black satin knee breeches remained the full dress style. They were worn very tight over a high boot with a strap underneath. Also, they beamed of striped, checked, and plaid fabrics in various colors, with the dashing coat usually in a solid color. Coats with a front closing flap gave way to buttons down the center and a side pocket design.

1830-1840

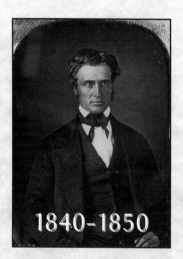
1840-1850

1851-1860

1861-1870

1861-1870

Frock coats became popular with matching vest, watch chain, and dark top hat. A stovepipe top hat was worn, and the slender coat gave away to an elaborately cut jacket. The tails were cut away to such an extent that it became the morning coat. The tails were also cut away from the waist at an angle to become the swallowtail.

Shawl collar vest, two pocket victorian era meant cravats and puff ties, satin and silk were common in men's attire.

1871-1880

High-crowned, curving-brimmed bowler hats became popular. A single-breasted morning coat or a double-breasted overcoat with a turned-down collar and small bow tie were common. Facial hair was common either a full beard or a groomed mustache.

Men in work attire would be seen in collarless checked flannel with four-button opening and a low-crowned derby. Canes came into style purely for show and stayed for a number of years.

1881-1890

Jackets turned to light-colored waistcoats with a dark cutaway and trousers. A wing collar and little bow tie were popular. A straw hat, a cane, and a chained pocket watch were common accessories. Shirts were of light colors, line checks and stripes. A hunting jacket style appeared with knickerbockers. Sleeve garters were a popular accessory. They were to hold long sleeves to the correct length, but also caught on as a fashion statement. Ready-made shirts all came in one length of sleeve—extra long.

1891-1900

A frock coat, with silk-faced lapels, was worn with a matching vest and finely checked trousers, though knickerbockers were still popular. Big polka-dot ties, with a wing collar was particularly popular. Mutton-chop whiskers were also seen. Hats were a mixture of bowling hats and driving caps. The popular fabric for jackets was tweed. Walking sticks or canes were popular. Many came with a hidden flask or compass built in. They were more of a fashion accessory than an actual walking aid. Dress gloves also accentuated the well-dressed man. Trousers did not have belt loops until the 20th century.

1901-1920

Informal clothing turned to easy-fitting lounge jackets with narrow lapels and single-breasted fastening, light colored trousers and shirts with a knotted tie. Hats were wore formally only. Gentlemen wore coats that had a narrow shape, with white shirts and high stiff collars. Accessories included a black bow tie or a narrow tie. They wore their hair short with large mustaches.

1921-1930

Fashion had a gangster influence. Though gangsters projected an image of businessmen, they didn't choose typical business colors and styles. They took every detail to the extreme. Their suits featured wider stripes, bolder plaids, colorful ties, pronounced shoulders, narrow waists, and wide trouser bottoms. They topped their extreme look with fedora hats in a wide variety of colors: almond green, dove, lilac, petrol blue, brown, and dark gray.

1871–1880

1881–1890

1891–1900

1901–1920

1921–1930

Organizing

After collecting stories, names, dates, locations, and photographs, it is time to get organized. Find a clean work area to spread out your finds. As you begin to accumulate photos and materials, organize and protect them in archival safe photo files and boxes. Use labeled file dividers to help divide photos into groups—by person, family, time-period, or life-stages.

Family Grouping

If you are working with a number of different family lines, sort by families then by years, places they have lived or events. Using a cabinet, file folders, or individual bins will help keep items separated in the initial sorting process.

Theme Grouping

A family scrapbook chronicles a theme such as a holiday tradition, a family occupation, or a memorable event. Organize the documents and photographs into piles that support the album theme you have chosen. If the theme is family war heroes, gather documents, pictures, and histories dealing with the various wars. Then organize the materials by wars, chronologically, or by families, depending upon your focus. Keep the group manageable.

Your pages are a continual work in progress depending on later pictures you find or more information you discover about a person, place, or event.

Focus group examples:
- the last four generations on your paternal side
- the history of the family members who carved a particular community
- experiences of ancestors who were explorers or pioneers
- the travels of your immigrant ancestors
- where your great grandparents lived, moved, and finally met
- occupations passed down through generations
- the medical and health conditions of men in the family over a few generations

Storing

Photographs are part of the historical record. It is imperative that originals are preserved. They are fragile. If you must handle a photograph, hold it only by the edge; on no account touch the surface. Even with clean fingers, natural oil secretions can damage a photo over time. Preferably wear clean, fine cotton gloves.

Don't throw any photos away even if they don't clean up or restore perfectly or you do not know who they are; they are still valuable historical documents.

Steps for storing photographs and important documents:

1. Once original photographs and documents are identified, copied, and recorded on the three research documents, safely store.

2. Since newspapers are made of highly acidic paper and deteriorate so quickly, photocopy the pertinent information onto acid-free paper. Then store the original paper in an acid-free box, or mount clippings in an archival scrapbook. Clippings can also be stored in acid-free file folders, interweaved with acid-free paper. If you want to frame the clipping, frame the acid-free copy rather than the original clipping.

3. Unroll any paper objects that have been stored rolled for many years. Because they may be quite brittle, moisture needs to be restored to the document. Place the document in a humid environment for several hours to make it more flexible. Then attempt to carefully unroll and flatten it. Do not proceed if it resists or begins to crack or tear.

Once the document is flat, place it between two pieces of blotting paper. Place a heavy object on top and let it set for a few days. Once the document is dry and flat, store it flat between two pieces of archival paper.

4. Place each individual image in a mylar or paper sleeve. Plastic sandwich bags are an inexpensive alternative to plastic sleeves.

Plastic enclosures are safe for documents ONLY if they are made of polyester, polypropylene, or polyethylene. Other plastics are not chemically stable and will release damaging acids over time. Especially dangerous is PVC (polyvinylchloride) commonly found in store-bought binders; it emits hydrochloric acid over time.

5. Use archival-safe photo boxes.

6. Create a filing system by the type of document or by the individual's name.

7. Do not store negatives in the same place as photographs. In the event something happens to the photos, the negatives will still be available to reprint.

8. Put articles in clean, chemically inert polyester bags or sleeves. Store articles in a cool, dry, storage area with minimal light, avoiding attics, garages, and basements.

9. Store documents flat. You may put more than one document in a sleeve but documents should be separated with acid-free paper to prevent acid migration from one document to another.

Scrapbooking Instructions

Heritage-type scrapbooks are more advanced than general scrapbooks. For purposes of this book, the author assumes the reader has a working knowledge of basic scrapbooking supplies and techniques. If the reader is unfamiliar with scrapbooking, it is suggested that she reviews a beginning scrapbook volume before continuing with this book.

Heritage scrapbooking consists of compiling, preserving, and sharing family traditions, stories, photos, and documents in an artistic way. Rather than just providing names and dates on a pedigree chart, your heritage can be shared in an beautiful way.

Scrapbooking Supplies

When scrapbooking family history, a number of the traditional scrapbooking supplies and tools are used. Most products on the market can be modified to work in a heritage forum. To stay authentic to the period, some modifications are necessary. For example, contemporary journaling tags can be aged with ink, embossing powders, or chalk.

When gathering materials together, you may run across a variety of documents, maps, and certificates. Do not use original items in your scrapbook. Copy items such as birth certificates, military records, even report cards.

Browse through back issues of magazines, dated copies of social etiquette books, or other publications containing illustrations from the time period you are scrapbooking. The publications of the day will give you a feel for color schemes that were popular as well as the "in" fashions, hairstyles, and tidbits of information to include in your layout design.

Supplies:
1. Scrapbooking papers in appropriate colors and designs
2. Adhesives
3. Archives markers
4. Embossing powder
5. Thin wire
6. Variety of inks
7. Appropriately colored fabric
8. Craft paint
9. Walnut ink
10. Glue sticks
11. Chalk
12. Archival spray
13. Store purchased stickers

Tools:

1. Sandpaper/steel wool
2. Brush
3. Sponge
4. Hole punch
5. Pliers/wire cutter
6. Decorative scissors
7. Laminator
8. Brush
9. Craft knife
10. Tweezers
11. Scissors
12. Distressing brush
13. Hammer
14. Sewing machine
15. Foam brush
16. Wax seal
17. Wood burner
18. Metal embosser
19. Crimper
20. Stamps
21. Ribbon punch
22. Paper cutter
23. Impact stamp
24. Dryer

Embellishments:

- Ribbons and fibers
- Antique buttons
- Jewelry
- Snap, buckles, zippers
- Eyelets, brads, snaps
- Paper clips
- Game pieces
- Slide mounts
- Tiles, cubes
- Metal hardware
- Small frames
- Leather fasteners
- Any other found objects which may enhance a scrapbook page without damaging the album

Scrapbooking Techniques

Since photos and documents are copied, the images may look better than they should for their age. A number of techniques can be used to age your photographs and ephemeral to match the proper era. Choose the desired technique(s) to distress and age your design.

Deacidfying

Due to the acidity in documents, newsprint, and books, these papers are prone to deteriorate over time.

Acid migration occurs when a low-quality paper bleeds onto neighboring pieces of paper. The best solution is to photocopy the information onto acid-free buffered paper. Then scrapbook with the photocopy.

If you choose to include an original document, use an acid-neutralizing archival preservation mist to deacidify the paper first. Spray both sides of the paper to protect the paper from deterioration and crumbling.

Sanding

When making copies of original old photographs, the images may no longer have an aged look. Depending on the amount of aging desired, there are a number of techniques one can use to distress the photographs.

Sanding copied photographs exposes the layers underneath the surface, giving an aged well-worn look. Randomly sanding photographs, adds power to any layout spreads dealing with disaster or troubled times.

Choose sandpaper, steel wool, or sanding block grit, depending on the severity of the aging desired.

Working on a protected surface, sand the edges. Work in a variety of directions. Once the edges are to your liking, lighting sand the entire image with an ultrafine-grit sanding block. Be careful not to damage the important images in the photo.

Further aging can be accomplished by chalking or inking the sanded edges.

Burning

The above photograph was distressed by burning. Touch a photo or piece of paper to a flame just long enough for the paper to be burned. Keep the flame in control by blowing it out before it burns more than desired. If the paper has been ripped, the thinner part of the paper will burn more quickly.

Chalking/Inking

The above cardstock was distressed with chalk and ink. The light brown chalk was applied with a makeup applicator and can be applied as heavily as desired. Chalk has a tendency to brush off and may not be as dark as ink.

The dark brown at the bottom of the cardstock was applied by running the paper edge over a brown ink pad. This gives a darker and more dramatic look than the chalk. It is also harder to control where the ink goes, leaving a rustic unpredictable look.

Wet Embossing

Embossing requires embossing ink and a heat source. Sprinkle embossing powder on the desired location. Using a low heating craft dryer, apply direct heat to the powder. Be aware of how close to the ink you are. If you are too far away the powder will not melt but blow the powder around instead. Get as close as possible without blowing the powder away. Let it cool and harden before continuing. Add more powder and reheat until you acquire the look you desire. You've heated it enough when the surface is smooth (not grainy) and glossy. If the surface of your embossing cracks, you've heated it too long. If it flakes or feels grainy, it needs to be heated a few moments longer.

Another option is to use a rubber stamp. Ink the stamp and apply to paper immediately. Sprinkle the embossing powder over the ink while it is still wet. Tap off excess powder. Apply heat for several seconds to completely melt the powder to the paper.

Staining

Staining produces an aged look. Experiment with coffee, tea, and walnut ink to find the color you desire.

Make a strong cup of coffee or tea. Place a paper item to be stained directly into the mixture, then remove it immediately and allow to dry on a protected surface. Coffee will produce a brown color while tea will leave a yellower color.

Ribbon, lace, and fabric may need to be soaked for up to an hour for the color to stain the fibers. The longer it remains in the solution the darker the material will stain. Allow the material to dry overnight.

To use walnut ink, mix granules with water to make a solutions as dark as desired. The longer paper or fabric is left in the walnut ink the dark it becomes. In the photo above, the papers have been stained different colors. The lightest color was left in the ink for 10 minute, the medium for 30 minutes and the darkest was left overnight.

The walnut ink solution can also be put in a spray bottle and misted of complete layouts and designs to add a subtle darkening.

Metal Engraving

A metal engraver produces small pulses on metal, leaving a clean line. Hold the engraver perpendicular and steady. Avoid pressing too hard while engraving. Keep the pressure consistent as you work.

Wood Burning

A wood burner actually burns markings into wood. Hold the burner at an angle as you would a pencil. Avoid pressing too hard while burning. Keep the pressure consistent as you work.

This tool can also be used to mark on leather. Regardless of the material, practice on a scrap piece before working on the project to determine the pressure and speed you desire.

Researching Instructions

Once you have exhausted your sources at home and the homes of relatives, and sorted your findings into categories, it is time to begin the research. Review what you have collected and organized thus far. Determine what you are lacking. List where most likely you would find such information. Then follow the steps below.

> When researching, focus on one step at a time:
> 1. Identify what you know.
> 2. Decide what you want to learn.
> 3. Choose a source to search.
> 4. Locate the source and record your findings.
> 5. Repeat steps 1–4.

Basic Sources

Begin your research at local community resources. Look for journals, family histories, and vital records. Many records that are held at the national level in government and private collections are often found also in your community on microfiche, microfilm, or computer websites. Libraries and archives in the United States are organized on city, county, state, and national levels.

Check with local genealogical and historical societies to see if they reflect your ancestors' ethnic or national background.

When gathering facts, remember complications and biographies are written by someone other than the subject. The writer may have heard the story, interviewed someone, or studied the facts, but it is still considered a secondary source. That is why it is important to search out and make contact with the oldest living relatives who may know stories and events first-hand. They may be your only source to a first-hand account of relations, conditions, activities, beliefs, and traditions.

Though the Library of Congress and the Family History Library in Salt Lake City are impressive when you first begin to search, it may be more helpful to look at the depositories locally first. Check the facilities near your home or in the local of your ancestors' homes. After exhausting these resources it is time to widen your searching area.

In association with the Family History Center in Salt Lake City, there are 1800 Family History Centers nationwide providing a nondenominational public service sponsored by the Church of Jesus Christ of Latter-day Saints. The family history libraries have access to the International Genealogical Index (IGI) which has more than 200 million names available to search, along with thousands of printed family records. To see what is available at the library before planning a visit check the inventory at www.familysearch.org.

Another nationally recognized resource for genealogist is the National Archives and Records Administration (NARA). This independent federal agency is responsible for preserving the nations' history by maintaining and managing federal records.

The system includes 13 regional branches of the National Archives and 12 presidential libraries. The Archives offer special publications, or General Information Leaflets (GILs) concerning records for genealogical research.

The Library of Congress as well as the National Archives has a strong site on the Internet that provides a variety of information.

Refer to Recommended Sources on page 126 for contact information for these departments and other helpful sites.

While discussing a wide variety of historical events in this book specific sources are given that pertain specially to that event. However, always check basic sources first.

Where Can I Find…?

If you need:	Primary sources:	Secondary sources:
Birth/death information	cemetery, church, military, probate, vital, family Bible	military, census, cemetery, newspaper, obituary, tax, land, town
Children's names & ages	church, family Bible, land, probate, vital	census, compiled history, immigration, obituary
Marriage information	family Bible, marriage certificate	journal, newspaper
Burial information	cemetery, death certificate	family Bible, family history
Where family lived	census, land, military, obituary	county history, newspaper
Family's religion	church, family Bible, cemetery	nationality

When Records Became Available

Records Type	YEARS			
	1600	1700	1800	1900
Home Sources	▬▬	▬▬	▬▬	▬▬
Civil Records			▬	▬▬
Church Records	▬▬	▬▬	▬▬	▬▬
Census Records		▬	▬▬	▬▬
Cemetery Records		▬▬	▬▬	▬▬
Military Records		▬	▬▬	▬▬
Land Records	▬▬	▬▬	▬▬	▬▬
Wills	▬▬	▬▬	▬▬	▬▬
Court Records	▬▬	▬▬	▬▬	▬▬
Immigration		▬	▬▬	▬▬

Census

Census records are federal, state, and local governments' attempt to obtain a complete listing of all citizens in the United States. Federal census are available from 1790 to 1920. Because of a 72-year privacy cap, the 1920 census is the most recent available to public research.

The National Archives and regional branches have compiled sets of all the federal censuses. Many large public libraries and most state libraries have at least the federal census pertaining to their regional area. Libraries with large genealogical collections may have the complete set of federal censuses as well as many of the indexes. Online some paid research websites are linked to the census records that you can view at a fee.

The information in the census may not be fool proof. A census taker walked from one house to another to count those living in different areas. It may have taken the taker weeks or months to cover a small area. A family member may have bounced between houses inadvertently missing the census taker both times she came missing being counted in either household. Or in the same scenario be counted twice. Or the person giving the information could be a neighbor visiting or one of the children that gave a wrong birth date or country their father originated from. There will be human errors.

Census information:

The United States census has been taken every 10 years. Each census contains different information depending on what data the government needed at that time.

1940-1970 census records are classified as confidential and are not available to the public.

1930 census records devoted one line to each individual listing
- name/age/sex/color/birth place
- relationship to head of household
- birth place of parents'
- education
- veteran facts
- employment information
- personal description

1920 census records devoted one line to each individual listing
- name/age/sex/color/birth place
- relationship to head of household
- parents' birth place
- education
- ownership of home
- employment information
- personal description
- nativity/mother tongue

1910 census records listed the
- name of everyone in the household
- age/sex/color/birth place
- relationship to head of household
- parents' birth places
- education
- ownership of home
- if anyone was a survivor of the Civil War
- employment information
- personal description

1900 census records listed the
- name of everyone in household
- age/sex/color/occupation/birthplace
- relationship to head of household
- parents' birth places

1890 census records were destroyed by fire in 1921

1880 census records list the
- name of everyone in household
- age/sex/color/birth place
- parents' names/birth places
- education
- occupations
- relationship of each person to head of household

1870-1850 census records list
- name/sex/color/birth place/age
- occupation
- family property value

1840-1800 census records list
- head of household by name
- everyone else listed by age/sex

1790 census records list
- name of head of household

Slave schedules list
- slaves in southern states between 1850-1860
- arranged in order by state and county
- the owner is the principal party named
- number of slaves
- slave's sex and age

Agriculture and manufacturing schedules provide
- land holdings
- how the land was being used
- what crops were grown
- what animals were on farm

Manufacturing schedules list:
- number of employees used
- type of items manufactured
- annual income

When working with a census record, print out a blank form for the census year you are reviewing. Blank census records can be downloaded from www.FamilySearch.org or www.Ancestry.com. Carefully transcribe the pertinent information about your family. Include the names of families living on either side of your relatives' home. These may later prove to be relatives or friends that have immigrated with your family. When you no longer can locate your family in census records, look for old neighbors' names which may lead you to where your family relocated.

Historical Events Timeline

(example 1600-2000)   Family name

1607–Jamestown settled
1618–48–Thirty Years' War
1619–First Negroes landed
1620–Mayflower Compact signed
1631–First newspaper published (Paris)
1635–Connecticut first settled
1642–46–English Civil War
1660–Pilgrims landed
1660–Composition of light discovered by Sir Isaac Newton
1665–Great plague in London
1666–Great fire of London
1675–1676–King Philip's War (Indian)
1681–Oil street lights used in London
1692–Salem Witch Trials
1709–Bartolomeo Cristofori invented the piano
1754–French and Indian War
1766–Stamp act repealed
1773–Boston Tea Party
1774–1st Continental Congress
1775–Paul Revere's ride
1776–Dec of Independence adopted
1787–Constitution completed
1789–George Washington 1st president
1791–1st US bank established
1794–Eli Whitney patents the cotton gin
1795–The preserving jar for food introduced
1796–John Adams 2nd president
1801–Thomas Jefferson 3rd president
1803–Louisiana Purchase
1804–Lewis/Clark expedition began
1807–Robert Fulton built first steamboat
1812–1815–War with Britain
1815–Battle of Waterloo between British and French–Napoleon defeated
1817–1825–James Monroe 4th president
1820–Missouri Compromise
1820–Maine/Missouri join Union
1820–Slavery spreads west
1823–First American settlement in Tejas (Texas)
1824–Creation of the Bureau of Indian Affairs

1600   *1700*   *1800*

When piecing together an ancestor's life, work chronologically. Using land, census, and tax records compile a simple chronological idea of where the generations of your family lived. Using the Historical Events Timeline Chart above or a similar chart, keep track of the movements of your family.

1829–Andrew Jackson 5th president
1830–The Indian Removal Act
1836–Texas independence from Mexico
1839–Discovery of photography
1840–Oregon Trail used
1844–First successful telegraph line set up
1846–1848–Mexican War
1846–Great Irish potato famine began
1847–Mormon pioneers in Salt Lake Valley
1848–Revolutions in Italy, France, Austria and Germany
1848–Discovery of Gold in California

1850–Fugitive Slave Law passed
1850–Levi Strauss made heavy weight trousers
1852–Franklin Pierce 6th president
1852–20,000 Chinese immigrants arrive looking for gold
1854–Crimean War
1856–James Buchanan 7th president
1859–Silver discovered in Virginia City, Nevada
1860–Pony Express begun
1861–1865–Civil War
1861–Abraham Lincoln 8th president
1862–Emancipation Proclamation
1862–Homestead act signed
1862–Transcontinental telegraph

1865–13th Amendment ends slavery
1865–Assassination of Abraham Lincoln
1865–Andrew Johnson 9th president
1867–Purchase of Alaska
1867–The first practical and modern typewriter invented
1868–14th Amendment–guaranteeing blacks civil rights
1868–Ulysses S. Grant 10th president
1868–J P Knight invents traffic lights
1869–First transcontinental railroad completed
1871–Great Chicago fire
1871–Barnum and Bailey opens Greatest Show on Earth
1873–Joseph Glidden invents barbed wire

1825	1850	1865

In the appropriate boxes above, list where your ancestors were living and what they were doing at certain times in history. This may put your ancestors' movements and actions into perspective for you.

Keep a journal or travel log of your family members. When and why did they move? Who traveled

Historical Events Timeline

(example 1800–1950)   Family name

1875—Civil Rights Act
1876—Bell patented the telephone
1876—Colorado enters Union
1877—Edison invented the phonograph
1877—Desert Land Act
1879—Edison invented incandescent light
1882—Chinese Exclusion Act
1883—Northern Pacific Railroad complete
1886—Statue of Liberty dedicated
1890—Copper mining driving Mexican Americans from their lands
1892—Ellis Island opened to immigrants
1894—Edison introduced motion pictures
1898–1899—Spanish–American War
1901—Theodore Roosevelt 11th president
1903—Wright Brothers' first flight
1904—Moving pictures established
1908—Henry Ford introduced Model T
1911—Mexican Revolution
1912—Titanic sank
1914—First national income tax
1917–1918—US involvement in WWI
1918—Influenza epidemic kills 22 million
1920—Women's right to vote
1920—Popularity of the radio increased
1921—KDKA first U.S. radio station
1923—First talking movies
1927—Charles Lindbergh soloed Atlantic
1928—Penicillin discovered
1929—Stock Market Crash
1929—Great Depression began
1933—Prohibition ended
1934—"Dust Bowl" drought
1935—Social Security Act
1936—Spanish (Spain) civil war
1937—Hindenburg exploded
1940—Churchill became prime minister
1941–1945—US involvement in WWII
1944—Ballpoint pen introduced

1875	1900	1925

with them? When you lose track of them, look at the birth places of their children. Then find them in the census records to get more infor-mation about the family and their doings. If a family member is miss-ing between census records look for other documents. Check for mar-riage licenses or death records.

Referring to the chart above, was there a war going on and was your relative of age to serve? If so check

1950–1953–Korean War
1953–USSR explodes their first hydrogen bomb
1954–TV dinners introduced
1954–Jonas Salk starts inoculating with antipolio serum
1957–Suez Canal
1961–Berlin wall up
1963–John F. Kennedy assassinated
1965–Vietnam war begins
1968–Woodstock

1976–VHS and Betamax introduced
1977–First flight of space shuttle
1981–Compact disks hit the market
1986–Laptop computers introduced
1991–World Wide Web
1998–First part of International Space Station launched

1950	1975	2000

war records of the period.

Was there a tragedy that would have caused them to relocate? Was there an invention that would have effected their livelihood? Did family members stay together or part ways due to the events happening?

Write in events in later dates that are of interest to your family.

Historical Events

Whenever a major event happens the "experts" are called in. They are asked "Why is this happening?" "What can you tell us so we understand the event?" The experts usually refer to history. They know that what happened historically affects current events and events tend to repeat themselves.

Throughout this book, different historical events are explained and the effect they had on a family or an individual. As you research your heritage and place your family into historical events, be certain to learn the outcome of the event and how it effected your family. Historic events are rarely isolated. Many events that we consider individual effect one another. Rarely did our ancestors want to be involved in the event. The activities going on around them usually determined where they moved, their occupation, where they lived, and many times who they married and with whom they associated.

As you study your family, examine why and how they did what they did. Their attitudes, health, religion, and affluence all have played a part and effected your life today.

Over the next few pages, Phebe Draper has been used as an example, showing how the events of the day determined her life's experiences. Ultimately her choices have effected hundreds of progenitors in their faith, beliefs, and lifestyles.

Ask questions about the event.
- Did your family relocate, change occupations, change religious beliefs, stay connected to family?
- Do you see similarities in the events of their lives and yours?
- If you were placed in the same event, would you have reacted in the same manner?
- Did they make a wise choice?
- How have their choices and actions effected your life?
- How are the choices you are making going to effect your progenitors?

Phebe Draper

My great grandmother, Phebe Draper joined the Church of Jesus Christ of Latter-day Saints in 1833 while living in Canada. She was compelled to uproot her family and move to Kirtland, Ohio with her seven small children. She was determined to meet Joseph Smith and hear from him directly what missionaries had told her in Canada. Phebe did meet Joseph and eventually traveled with the pioneers to the Salt Lake Valley.

Mormon Battalion

As the Mormon pioneers traveled across the plains, United States agents approached them and demanded that the men participate in the Spanish American War. The majority of able-bodied men gathered together under the name of the Mormon Battalion and fought from 1846 to 1848. My great grandmother, Phebe, her husband Ebenezer, and her son young Zemira were among the Battalion members. Phebe was one of four women in the battalion and served as the laundress.

After the war was over, the group disbanded and Phebe and family found themselves stranded in California.

Through further research, I found that Phebe's father and children had continued the trek with the other pioneers and arrived in the Salt Lake Valley. Had I not read her journal of the events she experienced on the trek, I would have assumed she and her husband and son had died along the way because they did not arrive in the Salt Lake Valley with the rest of her family. Rather than assuming they died along the way, I followed the events along the trail. There were no official records of this battalion as with other wars. There was no pensions given or military information kept. All the information I gathered was from journals kept by Battalion members.

Tip: On the back of a scrapbook page that shows a number of people, list names and relationships. For the layout above I made a drawing of where each person was standing and numbered them (see below). I then made a list identifying each person by number. Even if the photograph contains people that are not family members. This information may later help link neighbors to family members who were in the same settlement. When you stall in research, find your family's neighbors. These people may have traveled with your family or may give an accurate account of what your ancestor was experiencing by reading their journals and histories.

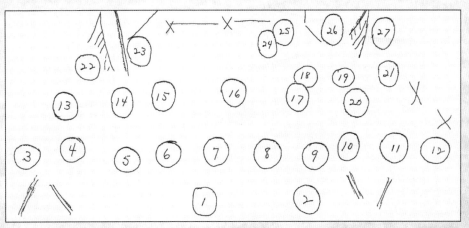

California Gold Rush

During the first three years of the California Gold Rush starting in 1847, over 200,000 people flocked to Sutter's mill to "strike it rich." Most of the men who came were disinherited sons, adventurers, or political undesirables. Keeping this fact in mind, this is a possible place to find relatives that show up missing in a census without a reason. These gold seekers are no longer living with their families because they have gone to California and there are no records of this move other than journals and letters. Try to locate any letters or journals left by the family member. Read through old historical texts about the gold rush to see if a name is recognizable to you.

When the Mormon Batallion disbanded, Phebe found herself in California, hundreds of miles from her children. The government offered no help in uniting the Battalion members with their families. Phebe and her husband and son worked in the California gold mines to earn enough money to travel to Utah.

Once Phebe had finally arrived in the Salt Lake Valley, she found that her father and children had settled on a piece of land south of Salt Lake City named Draper after her father William Draper.

Mormon Money

Most of the Mormon pioneers arrived in the Salt Lake valley with no cash because all such means had been used to purchase wagons, oxen, and food for their journey west. It is estimated that among the entire company of Mormons who entered the Great Salt Lake Valley on 24 July 1847, there was less than one dollar per person. This comprised the entire money supply in the Utah territory at that time.

The gold dust brought from the California goldfields was used in lieu of money. This medium was awkward when transporting the dust and some dust was being lost every time it was weighed.

The pioneers began operation of the Deseret Mint in November of 1848 using the gold dust to make the coins. When the time came that they did not have enough coins to meet the demand, they begun issuing paper currency.

As communication and transportation in the country improved, the coins and currency of the United States gradually became more plentiful throughout the Utah Territory and the need for locally produced coinage diminished. On Feb. 26, 1862, the mint was closed. A few of the rare gold coins minted by the pioneers still exist but are very rare and normally housed in museums.

Deseret Alphabet

When Phebe arrived in the Salt Lake Valley she came into a community filled with immigrants. People from around the world had made their way to Salt Lake seeking religious freedom. With the great influx of foreign speaking people, the valley developed a simplified language that all could use to communicate. The Deseret Alphabet developed by the University of Deseret in 1854 was 38 characters which translated to basic words used to communicate. The new phonetic system offered the following advantages:
- It demonstrated cultural exclusiveness, which at the time was important to the pioneers.
- It kept secrets from curious non-Mormons.
- It controlled what children were allowed to read.
- It eliminated the awkward problem of phonetic spelling.
- It helped acclimate immigrants and a variety of languages and dialects arriving in the valley.

Since it was so expensive to translate and convert books and learning aids into the new language, the alphabet did not last long. Eventually the language died out and the majority of the residents learned the English language.

Though the above layouts do not specifically deal with a family member, they work well in telling the story of Phebe. They show the conditions of the day and the events experienced by Phebe as she traveled to Utah. It also gives a better understanding of the time period and what the Pioneers were experiencing with their new lifestyle.

Movement

One of the primary tools in learning about your family is learning where they lived and why they moved. A large part of your ancestors history is movement. War, religion, economics, and more shaped the events of the day. Working backwards in time, find where and why they relocated. In most cases, your ancestors did not want to move. They preferred to stay close to family for the comfort of helping hands. They also were familiar with the typography and followed in the footsteps and livelihood of their fathers. The migration to America is what usually comes to mind when speaking on migration. There are a myriad of reasons your ancestors migrated to America.

The first places to look for movement is in journals. This may also tell the emotional side of the move and the families reactions. Were they excited, hesitant, ready, scared? Who migrated with them?

Read books and keep extensive notes on the places your ancestors came from and what was happening at the time they lived there and at the time they left.

- What was their occupation?
- Did it have to change?
- Did extended family move with them?
- What were they looking for?
- Did they find it?

When your ancestors arrived, they prefered to settle in places where the land was similar to what they were familiar with in their motherland. A fisherman by trade settled by the ocean, while a farmer looked and settled on fertile ground. They also settled near people of like morals and standards.

The following pages show a few of the reasons your ancestors may have moved or relocated. Some events are found prominently in high school history books while others are not as familiar. As you look at these examples, let your mind be sparked as to where your family was at the time. How was your family effected by the same or similar events?

When historians think about what causes migration, they think of "push" and "pull" factors. Something pushes people out of one place—a drought or perhaps an invasion—and something "pulls" them to another place—often available land or jobs. The migration might be a short distance,from the countryside to nearby cities, or great distances across continents or oceans.

It is easier to track and document a migration between countries because nations have historically taken a deep interest in people who cross national borders. Paperwork is filed, and immigrants are often carefully counted and scrutinized. But internal migrations, although more difficult to track, can be just as important.

Migration involves groups of people—families, neighbors, and entire villages who traveled together. Some in mass, while small groups followed from the same area. Part of the "pull" effect of migration is the influence migrants had on friends and relatives back home to join them. Migrations typically involve large numbers of people, and last years if not decades.

The transformation of agriculture was a major "push" factor. People had been leaving farming for decades by the 1930s because for many farming was a sure route to poverty. Too many families pressed on using a limited amount of land; the typical farm shrank in size decade by decade after the Civil War, and the typical farmer by the 1930s was not a landowner but a tenant farmer or sharecropper who tended someone else's land and was unable to climb out of debt. To make matters worse, a rural depression had afflicted agriculture since the early 1920s and only worsened with the onset of the Great Depression in the 1930s. Declining agricultural prices year after year for over a decade drove even more sharecroppers to the cities and towns in search of better paying employment. Jobs and the possibility of a higher standard of living "pulled" people to the cities and towns of the South and northward.

During the past 300 years, wars, financial collapses, religious persecutions, disasters, famine, and disease have forced people to leave their homes and migrate to America. The United States, perhaps more than any other country in the world, is a land of immigrants.

Researching Movements

The movement of families and friends can be found by reviewing different documents.

Census records

Families and friends regularly traveled and settled together. A census may show a group of people moving between census records to a new location but they have all stayed together.

Land records

Check land records in the area you know they lived to see when they arrived, what they intended to find, and who they lived near.

Oral interviews

Oral interviews are helpful in getting a starting point. An older relative may remember that her father came west from Alabama and she may know the reason for the move.

Vital records

The movement of families can also be found in vital records. Follow birth records of the children, marriage, and divorce records of the couple for places they would have lived. Also look for birth and death records and obituaries in small town newspapers, wills, and immigration records.

Reasons for Migrating to the United States

1585
- The first group came from England, but sadly their settlement failed.

1607-1830
- Religious tolerance
- Rulers chose what church they wanted in their lands.
- English came to find gold
- During the 1600s and 1700s, wars ravaged Germany.
- Explore
- Claim land for their country
- Famines spread over Germany.
- Taxes, levied to pay for war
- Religious disputes
- Better job - more money
- Political freedom
- Political refugees fear for their lives
- Forced immigration such as slavery
- Family reunification
- Fleeing crop failure
- Famine

1830-1890
- Land and job shortages
- Rising taxes
- Land plentiful/inexpensive
- Jobs abundant/labor scarce
- Decline in birthrate/ increase in industry/urbanization
- Word of mouth that in America, the streets were, "paved with gold"
- Large numbers left Ireland following the Great Potato famines of 1845–47
- In 1872, large numbers left German territories impelled by rural poverty and periodic crop failures.

1890-1924
- Jews came for religious freedom
- Italians and Asians came for work
- Russians came to escape persecution
- Protection from WWI

1925–2000
- Protection from WWII
- Increased industry
- Freedom for Haitians/Cubans
- From Japan for economic growth
- China sought world control

Mayflower

On 6 Sep 1620, the Mayflower crossed the Atlantic with 101 passengers and the crew of about 30. Two babies were born aboard. One person died. Tools, furniture, barrels of salted beef, casks of butter, hogsheads of beer, dogs, pigs, and chickens were on board. Scurvy ran rampant. Although accounts are few, they all mentioned the troubled crossing, at one point even questioning the chances of successfully reaching America.

After eight weeks at sea, the passengers saw land that their maps called Cape Cod. They disembarked but found the area too sandy for crops. They searched up the coast until 21 Dec 1620 when they stepped onto land already named Plymouth by explorer John Smith.

Since they were no longer settling where they had thought, and did not technically have the permission of the King of England, the Pilgrims drew up the "Mayflower Compact," to give themselves the authority to establish a government—it was a temporary solution, until an official patent could be obtained.

Researching early ships

Ship manifests list those who traveled on a particular ship. To find whether or not your relative was on the Mayflower or a later ship and joined the Pilgrims in those first few years check the internet. If you know the time period or where they were traveling from, check the ship manifests. Using a website such as Ancestry.com or FamilySearch.org type in the name of the ship you feel they may have sailed. The Family History Library also has a passenger list on most ships on microfiche. There are also numerous websites you can pay a fee to look at various ship manifests. Using a search engine type in the name of the ship or search through immigration websites.

It would also be helpful to find a family history on the family members traveling. This may shed some light on why they left their native country and how they felt about the trip.

Mayflower Compact 1620

IN THE NAME OF GOD, AMEN. We, whose names are underwritten, the Loyal Subjects of our dread Sovereign Lord King James, by the Grace of God, of Great Britain, France, and Ireland, King, Defender of the Faith, &c. Having undertaken for the Glory of God, and Advancement of the Christian Faith, and the Honour of our King and Country, a Voyage to plant the first Colony in the northern Parts of Virginia; Do by these Presents, solemnly and mutually, in the Presence of God and one another, covenant and combine ourselves together into a civil Body Politick, for our better Ordering and Preservation, and Furtherance of the Ends aforesaid: And by Virtue hereof do enact, constitute, and frame, such just and equal Laws, Ordinances, Acts, Constitutions, and Officers, from time to time, as shall be thought most meet and convenient for the general Good of the Colony; unto which we promise all due Submission and Obedience.

IN WITNESS whereof we have hereunto subscribed our names at Cape-Cod the eleventh of November, in the Reign of our Sovereign Lord King James, of England, France, and Ireland, the eighteenth, and of Scotland the fifty-fourth, Anno Domini; 1620.

Signers

John Carver
William Bradford
Edward Winslow
William Brewster
Isaac Allerton
Myles Standish
John Alden
John Turner
Francis Eaton
James Chilton
John Craxton
John Billington
Moses Fletcher
John Goodman
Samuel Fuller
Christopher Martin
William Mullins
William White
Richard Warren
John Howland
Steven Hopkins
Digery Priest
Thomas Williams
Gilbert Winslow
Edmund Margesson
Peter Brown
Richard Britteridge
George Soule
Edward Tilly
John Tilly
Francis Cooke
Thomas Rogers
Thomas Tinker
John Ridgdale
Edward Fuller
Richard Clark
Richard Gardiner
John Allerton
Thomas English
Edward Doten
Edward Liester

George Soule

In 1620, the Mayflower prepared to set sail for America. Before the Mayflower left Europe, Pastor William Brewster asked the passengers "Are you willing to leave behind your friends? Can you and your children face the dangers of crossing the ocean? Are you ready to learn new ways of making your living? What if your families are attacked by wild natives?" The answer was "Our trust is in God alone. We must be free to worship the Lord in purity and truth, no matter what it may cost us."

Edward and Elizabeth Winslow were among the passengers. They brought with them my 10th great grandfather, George Soule. He was listed on the passengers list as the 21-25 year-old apprentice of Governor Edward Winslow. He later became the 35th signer of the Mayflower Compact.

In 1638, George sold his property at Plymouth and with Myles Standish and others moved across the bay to Duxbury where he was one of the town's founders.

George outlived almost all of the Pilgrims. A gourd belonging to him can be seen today in Memorial Hall in Plymouth. Through further research on the Mayflower Compact, I found George's actual signature. This brought the journey of the Mayflower more to life for me.

George Soule Sr.

Did you know?

Henry Wadsworth Longfellow descended from eight Mayflower passengers: William and Mary Brewster and their son Love Brewster; Richard Warren; John Alden; William and Alice Mullins and their daughter Priscilla. When the poet wrote, *The Courtship of Miles Standish*, it was based on the love story between his ancestors John Alden and Priscilla Mullins.

Pilgrims

The Pilgrims began as a religious group who felt that the only way to practice their religion was to separate from the Church of England.

These "Separatists" centered around Scrooby, England. They obtained a ship called the "Mayflower" and provisions for a long journey, they (102 passengers and about 30 sailors) set sail, in the autumn of 1620, and headed westward toward the new world.

For 65 days, the Pilgrims journeyed. The Mayflower was driven off course by heavy storms while heading for a settlement in Virginia and sought shelter in Cape Cod Bay at Provincetown (Massachusetts).

Between 1620 and 1630 a "Mayflower," or "Mayflowers," crossed the seas three times. The one in 1620 carried the Pilgrim Fathers to New Plymouth; one in 1629 carried Higginson's party to Salem; and one in 1630 carried Winthrop's party to Charlestown. The name Mayflower for ships was uncommonly common, with numerous ships of that name trading from numerous ports abroad. Besides the Mayflower, a number of early ships brought Pilgrims to the colonies.

In 1605, fifteen years before the Pilgrims came, Squanto went to England with an explorer named John Weymouth. There he learned to speak English. In England, Squanto met Samoset of the Wabanake Tribe, who had also left his native home with an English explorer. They returned together to Patuxet in 1620. When they arrived, the village was deserted. Everyone in their village had died from an illness the English slavers had left behind. Squanto and Samoset went to stay with a neighboring village of Wampanoags.

One year later, Squanto and Samoset were hunting near Patuxet. They were startled to see people in this deserted village. It was the Pilgrims. For several days, they observed the newcomers. Finally they approach the Pilgrims.

The Pilgrims were living in dirt-covered shelters. The wheat they brought with them would not grow in the rocky soil and there was a shortage of food. Nearly half of them had died during the winter.

Squanto stayed with the Pilgrims for the next few months and taught them how to survive in this new place. He was originally from the village of Patuxet, which once stood on the exact site where the Pilgrims built Plymouth. He brought them deer meat and beaver skins. He taught them how to cultivate corn and other new vegetables and how to build Indian-style houses. He pointed out poisonous plants and showed how other plants could be used as medicine. He explained how to dig and cook clams, how to get sap from the maple trees, use fish for fertilizer, and dozens of other skills needed for their survival.

Researching Pilgrims

There are numerous books and internet sites listing passengers, routes, and information about the

pilgrim ships. You may be able to determine which ship your ancestors traveled on by finding the date they arrived in America, the reason they left their native land, or what events were happening at the time.

William Bradford, the Pilgrims' principal leader, left the most comprehensive first-hand account of the Pilgrims. Bradford began recording his experiences in 1630 as a history to be passed down to his family. To see if your family is included on any of these ships look for journals or histories written by or about your relatives. If no record is found, read the information found about other pilgrims. There may be a journal entry by someone not related to you but they have mentioned your relative as someone who traveled with them.

> ### Early pilgrim ships
> A partial list is as follows:
> - Ann
> - Bonaventure
> - The Christian
> - The Diligent
> - Elizabeth
> - Elizabeth & Ann
> - Encrease
> - Fortune
> - Griffin
> - Handmaid
> - Hercules
> - Hopewell
> - James
> - John & Dorothy
> - Little James
> - Mayflower
> - Planter
> - Talbot
> - The Supply

Samuel and Jane Fuller

Edward Fuller, his wife, and his son Samuel came to America on the Mayflower. They had lived in Leyden, Holland for a short period of time, but originally came from Redenhall, Norfolk, England.

Edward's father was a butcher by trade, and his brother Samuel was a doctor and deacon. Edward's occupation, however, remains unknown. He and his wife both died the first winter in the new world.

Their son, Samuel who was 10 years old when traveling on the Mayflower, married Jane Lothrop, daughter of Rev. John Lothrop on April 1635. Jane had come to America from England with her father to escape the Queen of England's ban on their religious freedoms.

Did you know?

Thanksgiving Day is a historical, national, and religious holiday that began with the Pilgrims. After the survival of their first colony through a bitter winter, and the gathering of the harvest, Gov. William Bradford of Plymouth Colony issued a thanksgiving proclamation in the autumn of 1621. This first thanksgiving lasted three days, during which the Pilgrims feasted on wild turkey, venison, and vegetables with their Indian guests.

Days of thanksgiving were celebrated sporadically until, on Nov. 26, 1789, President George Washington issued a proclamation of a nationwide day of thanksgiving. He made it clear that the day should be one of prayer and giving thanks to God. It was to be celebrated by all religious denominations, a circumstance that helped to promote a spirit of common heritage.

President Abraham Lincoln's proclamation in 1863, designating the last Thursday in November as the day of celebration.

Emigration

If you are living in America and unless you are from Native American ancestors, your relatives would have emigrated from somewhere and immigrated to somewhere in the United States. There were reasons why your ancestors left their familiar location and migrate here.

It is important to study the history of both the place of departure and the destination in order to better understand the rationale behind your ancestors' decisions to move.

Search for your family members in U.S. records before looking in foreign records. You are more likely to find an immigrant's birthplace or last foreign residence in American records. Exhaust all American resources before searching in sources for other countries.

Sources to check for motherland

- census records
- naturalization papers
- citizenship records
- church records
- military records
- vital documents
- newspaper articles
- obituaries
- biographies
- immigration records
- citizenship papers

Reasons for emigrating

- Religious persecution
- Ethnic persecution
- Natural disasters
- Famine
- Economic problems
- Financial opportunity
- War or military service
- Political strife/oppression
- Following family/friends
- Escaping relatives
- Adoption
- Incarceration/deportment
- Slavery forced relocation

Researching Emigration Records

To find where your relatives emigrated from, start with what you know. Study immigration documents and census records. These documents may list where your ancestors originated from, the ship they were on, date they arrived, who traveled with them, their age at the time of arrival, their occupation, and reason for coming to a new country. If there are discrepancies, continue to research until you are satisfied with the information.

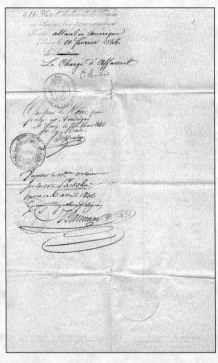

This Swiss emigration visa of Johann and Menga Conzett includes passenger info, destination, physical description of Johann and bears a wax seal of the issuing agency in charge. The back side of the document shows the French embassy's seal and permission to travel to and sail from a French port, the seal of the harbormaster of le Hávre, France as they departed, and the seal of the port police at New Orleans as they arrived in America.

Albert Einstein

Einstein was born in Germany, spending his boyhood in Munich. His teachers thought him stupid, because Einstein did not observe the petty rules of school. The boy liked to daydream and soar into the realms of his thought. The budding genius, at the age of 14, taught himself integral calculus and analytic geometry.

In 1894, Einstein's family moved to Italy. Young Albert was sent to Switzerland to study. He later became a Swiss citizen. He earned a PhD in physics from the University of Zurich.

His first job was as an inspector in the Swiss patent office. This paid the bills and gave him time to figure out the nature of the universe. His ideas revolutionized our entire understanding of the universe. His fundamental contribution was the theory of relativity and the formulation $E=MC^2$, which describes the relationship between mass and energy.

In 1921, he was awarded the Nobel Prize for his research of the photoelectric effect.

Einstein, who was Jewish, fled Germany just as Hitler came to power. On his arrival to the United States in 1933, Einstein had a job waiting for him. He was granted a lifetime professorship at Princeton. He was naturalized in 1940 as a U.S. citizen, which was his third citizenship.

Tip:

If you do not know where or when your family emigrated to the United States, design a page to represent your family members who traveled the ocean to a new land. The above page was made with a photograph of an unknown immigrant family. As you find more information about your relatives this page can be updated with the new information. In the meantime, you are reserving a place—a reminder to yourself to find that link across the ocean.

Immigration

It is common for Americans to find immigrant ancestors within three generations. Between 1840 and 1860 more than 200,000 immigrants arrived in America each year. Thousands of English, Dutch, Irish, and Scandinavian farmers and workers made the voyage to escape poverty and starvation. German thinkers and writers came to avoid political persecution.

Depending on where your ancestors settled in America, may be helpful in finding where they were from. It may help to refer to soil maps. Your ancestors knew how to grow particular crops. When they emigrated to a new area, they looked for a region similar to their old home in terms of terrain, soil, and vegetation. The agricultural schedules of the census will help you learn what crops your ancestors grew. Using a map when working with census records is imperative. Since the information is collected through the county and town limits, it would be hard to visualize and find your family without a map of their current times.

Migration patterns are helpful to review when you lose track of a your family due to a move. Refer to conditions they are already familiar with or types of people they are such as nationality or religious.

Researching Immigration Records

Search for your family members in U.S. records before looking in foreign records. You are more likely to find an immigrant's birthplace or last foreign residence in American records.

Consider immigration patterns. Your ancestors may not have boarded a ship in their home country. For example, the famous Von Trapp family was Austrian, but to escape the Nazis, they traveled to Italy before boarding a ship to America. Your ancestors may also have stopped in other countries on the way to America. It was not uncommon the stay in a boarding country long enough to get funding for passage. Some families worked their way onto a ship by working in different countries until they could afford to go. Some families were separated by sending family members whenever they had the money and opportunity for someone to go. These "layovers" may have been a day, month, year, or even a generation. It is important to consider the different aspects of your ancestors' journey and take into account any common circumstances they may have experienced.

Researching Naturalization Records

Naturalization is the legal procedure by which an alien becomes a citizen of a new country. Every nation has different sets of rules that determine citizenship. Under the Basic Naturalization Act of 1906,

naturalization forms became standardized and were sent to the U.S. Bureau of Immigration (later the Immigration and Naturalization Service [INS]) for examination. The formalized process required that a prospective citizen file a declaration of intention in which he or she renounced allegiance to foreign sovereignty. Following a waiting period of five years, an immigrant could then petition a federal court for formal citizenship.

> ## Naturalization records include:
> - Applicant's name
> - Birth date and place
> - Port and date of departure
> - Port and date of arrival
> - Last foreign address
> - Court location and date of petition or oath of allegiance
> - Physical description

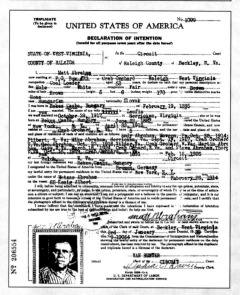

Declaration of Intention

Andrew Carnegie

Andrew was born in Scotland. Hard times and politics drove the Carnegie family from Scotland to America in 1848. The Carnegies had heard encouraging reports from America. "This country's far better for the working man than the old one," assured Andrew's aunt, who had lived in America for the last eight years. The Carnegies auctioned all their belongings only to find that they still did not have enough money to take the entire family on the voyage. They managed to borrow the last of the money and found room on a small sailing ship. At the harbor in Glasgow, they were assigned tightly squeezed bunks in the hold. It would be a 50 day trip with no privacy and miserable food. Once in America they took a steamer then a canal boat to Pittsburgh, where Andrew would eventually build his fortune.

After early struggles, he established the Carnegie Iron Works. He made a fortune, and gave significant gifts to educational work and free libraries.

The matchbook in the above right picture has a photograph of Andrew Carnegie on the front. I have written his immigration story–rags to riches in this booklet. This matchbook element can be easily stored in the plastic sleeve with the scrapbook and removed when one wants to read the complete story.

Did you know?

Many immigrant families depended on their children, relying on the speed with which children learned English, but also on their children's earning capabilities. Rural and urban children were employed in various sectors of the economy, from side jobs like peddling gum and newspapers or shining shoes to working in textile mills, factories and farms. In cities throughout Wisconsin, immigrant children worked in the brewing and textile industries, as well as in workshops, bakeries and butcher shops which were often family owned.

In mid nineteenth century Milwaukee, young girls often went into domestic service at the age of eleven or twelve. From 1870-1900, the number of children between the ages of ten and fifteen who were employed more than doubled from 750,000 to 1,750,000, and many of these children were immigrants. In rural Wisconsin, immigrant children and succeeding generations of children assisted their parents on the family farm.

Ship Passage

Researching Passenger Lists

Passenger lists were prepared by ship's masters from 1820 to 1900.

If your ancestor was a crew member he may have jumped ship at the new location and not returned to sail the ship back.

Researching Passenger Lists

We are all descended from immigrants. Whether they came to America in prehistoric times via the Bering Strait or later on ships, or airplanes, at some point in history, every person's ancestors came from somewhere else. Every American hoping to link generations and reach back in time will ultimately be faced with immigration questions. Fortunately, in modern times, the origins of most immigrants are documented in a wide variety of sources.

In 1819, the United States Congress enacted legislation to regulate the transport of passengers from foreign ports to the United States. As a provision of this act, ships' captains were required to submit a list of passengers to the collector of customs in the district in which the ship arrived. These passenger lists comprise the vast majority of immigration records. The content of passenger lists has changed significantly over the years and information is sparse on earlier lists.

The National Archives have originals, copies, or abstracts for a number of ship records.

Most records begin in 1891. Many early immigrations are not well documented, but some have been published.

Tip: Copy name of ship and the manifest including your family names. Secure a picture of the ship if possible.

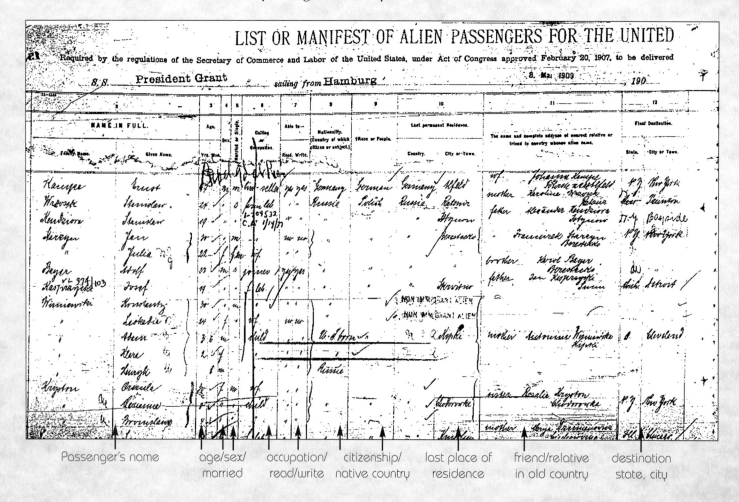

| Passenger's name | age/sex/ married | occupation/ read/write | citizenship/ native country | last place of residence | friend/relative in old country | destination state, city |

Thomas Hennessey

At 12 years old, Thomas left an abusive home life in England to find a new life. He stowed away on a ship bound for America. As far as anyone knows he had no further contact with his family in England.

He arrived in Mason, Texas about 1872–73. His exact age is in doubt since he recorded in his family bible that he was born 19 Oct 1855 but in the 1900 US Census he gives the date as October 1849 and in the 1910 US Census he gives it as Oct 1853 while on his headstone is recorded 19 Oct 1856. Efforts to obtain a birth certificate from England for him have been in vain, though nine English birth certificates for children named Thomas Hennessey between the years 1847 and 1860 have been obtained, not one of them was born on 19 Oct.

I have yet to find him in any immigration or emigration records. He never learned to write, so there is little written information about him or his life experience. This stowaway story would be lost had an inquiring granddaughter not been curious about her heritage.

Tip:
Take questions and stories such as Thomas' to a family reunion to see if anyone has found proof to validate this story or has found where he originated from or the names of his parents.

In 1868, Thomas Hennessey left home at age 12 and stowed away on a boat from England to America. His sister cried from the shore as she watched the ship sail away. Thomas never saw any of his family members again.

He never learned to read or write. His signature was simply an X.

Thomas became a rancher in Texas. In 1874, he married Matilda Martin in Texas. They had 10 children before they divorced in 1902. He lived until he was 71 years old.

Did you know?

Sometimes your ancestor may not be found in the immigration records. This may be for a number of reasons. He may have been sick upon arrival to the new country and sent back leaving his family in the new world. Review later immigration records or census records to see when he finally arrived.

He may have stowed away on a ship because he could not afford passage. He may have changed his name to hide from the reason he left his native land. His name could have been spelled in a fashion that you do not recognize. He may have been part of the crew and jumped ship. Research the emigration records before rechecking the immigration records to find when he left his home country. Information such as this can only come from family journals.

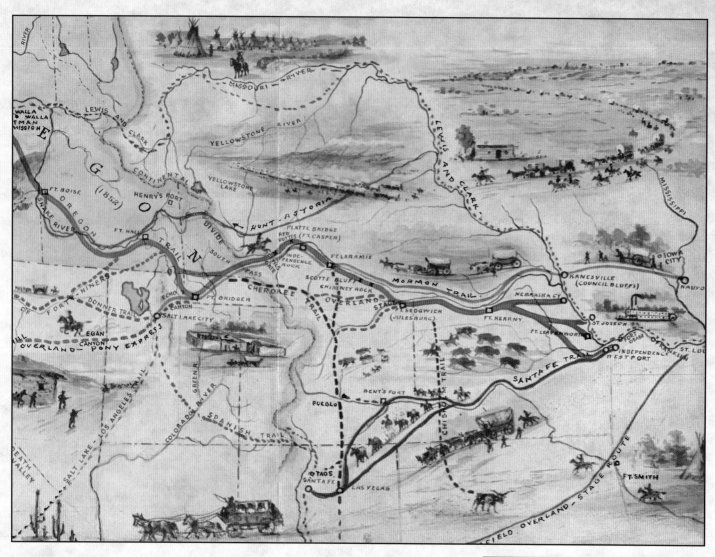

Western Migration

Migration was sometimes done in multiple steps. The Pilgrims first immigrated to the Netherlands and became more organized as a community before sailing to America. Our ancestors likewise may have immigrated to Canada because the ship's passage was less expensive to Halifax than to Philadelphia and then moved south into the United States at a later date. Study the history of both the place of departure and the destination to better understand the rationale behind your ancestors' moves.

Many of the original trails across the United States were formed as groups traveled westward. The Oregon Trail, Bozeman Trail, and Santa Fe Trail, were a few of the most notable. Some were taken to escape religious persecution while others were to explore or find riches. These original trails played an important part in the routes taken westward for generations after.

Reasons for westward migration:
- 1803 Louisiana Purchase—land available
- Mormons evicted from Nauvoo
- 1840–1846 Emigrants head to Oregon for land
- 1849-1860 California gold rush
- 1859 Colorado gold rush
- 1869 Transcontinental railroad completed
- 1870-1890 African-American move to Kansas to homestead

Edward Hennessey

Ed Hennessey and Lillie Adams eloped in 1901 because Lillie's parents did not approve of the new son-in-law. Her parents had been wealthy land and slave owners of the South just one generation past.

Though the Adams' financial situation had changed after the Civil War, their view concerning the marriage of Lillie, whose ancestors had been in America since the 1600s, to the son of a penniless recent immigrant from England, was not favorable.

After the marriage, the relationship between families became more strained. Ed eventually moved his family away from Texas. The family traveled alone, uncertain what to expect. Ed traded his home for a covered wagon. He built a chuckbox on the back that opened into a table. The wagon was supplied with several cast iron Dutch ovens, bedding, clothes, and an organ.

They settled in Arizona. Lillie's parents, convinced that she could do better, continued to beg her to come home and to at least "save" the children from such an awful lifestyle. Almost a hundred years later, Ed and Lillie's progenitors still live in Arizona.

Did you know?

Don't you wonder how this family got their photograph taken being out in the middle of no where and certainly without money?

These photographs were taken by a traveling photographer who made his money by documenting the events of the day.

Photographers such as this have been invaluable in documenting what life was like decades ago.

61

Mormon Pioneers

A Utah pioneer is defined as someone who came to the Utah Territory, died crossing the plains, or was born in the Utah Territory before 10 May 1869 which was the date of the connection of the East and West railroads.

Researching Pioneers

• Learn as much as you can about your ancestor. The more you know the more successful your research will be.

• Determine the approximate time your ancestor emigrated. If you know the exact departure date and/or arrival date you can quickly learn information about the trip.

• Start your search by seeing if your pioneer is already listed in Mormon Pioneer Search at www.familysearch.org. If the name is not found, try variations on the name spelling and expand the range of years that are searched.

• If you have identified the name with an entry in the index then verify the name by checking the name against a roster list.

• Reference the Pioneer Companies page or the book, Mormon Pioneer Companies Crossing the Plains and looking up the company name and then look for the source of the roster. You can then look up the roster (if it exists) in Journal History or the Deseret News.

If you are unable to find your ancestor in the Utah Immigration Index, search the Utah Census for 1850, 1860, and 1870. If you find them in the 1850 or 1860 census you can assume that they were a pioneer. If they are found in the 1870 census they may have been a pioneer as the cut off year is 1868 after that they may not have walked across the plains as the railroad came through Ogden (about 35 miles north of Salt Lake City) in May of 1869, which allowed the Saints to take the train across the country without the need of a wagon train.

It should be noted that many companies did not have an official roster. If there was no roster then link your ancestor with the company through other accounts of the trip prior to their leaving the Midwest. Some of these sources include personal diaries and journals and accounts by historians.

Read articles written by those associated with the Daughters of the Utah Pioneers.

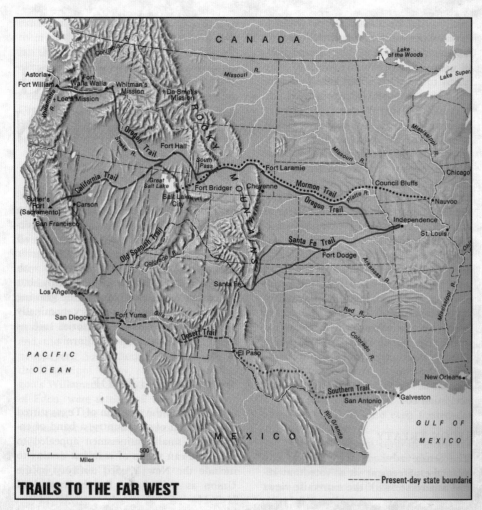

TRAILS TO THE FAR WEST

------- Present-day state boundarie

Before the completion of the railroads, emigrants and settlers traveled West in cross-country wagon trains. The 2,000-mile journey from Missouri to the West Coast took over four months to complete. Indians, sickness, and foul weather were only some of the dangers to early pioneers.

In 1866, shortly after leaving Denver this wagon train (shown top right) was attacked by hostile Indians.

Seeking promised fertile land, pioneers started life out in western frontier towns such as Independence, Missouri. Facing draught, floods, disease, looters, hostile Indians, dangerous animals, and dry mountainous terrains, many families saw their loved ones perish as they slowly traveled the Oregon Trail.

The strain of traveling the trail shows on this unidentified family (bottom right).

Pioneers, many who walked the entire 2,000 miles, followed the rivers in hopes of reaching Oregon, California, Utah, or some place where they could claim their homestead and start a new life.

WE HONOR OUR PIONEERS

Nils E Flygare

In 1864, my great grandfather Nils left his native land of Sweden for Liverpool then to the United States. He sailed on "Monarch of the Sea" with 1000 other immigrants bound for Utah. The passengers arrived in New York. There they began their trek westward. They traveled to Missouri by rail, then to Nebraska by river steamer where Brigham Young sent a wagon team from Utah to retrieve them.

Nils returned to Sweden to serve a two year mission. He then returned to Utah. In 1877, he was called again as a missionary to the Scandinavian Mission, where he translated and published the Book of Mormon in Swedish. His acts of compassion between the two countries led to his nickname "the Swedish Prince."

Did you know?

Some pioneers made the trip across the country multiple times. Some returned east to pick up family members left behind. Some traveled back to help struggling handcart groups. Some men were called on missions in the eastern states. While others traveled back to their native lands to help families and friends make the trek to Utah. Some made the trek more than once for numerous reasons.

63

Railroads

To connect railroad lines from coast to coast, work was started advancing the Central Pacific and the Union Pacific railroad lines. The crews of both railroad companies wanted to get further than the other. The workers lived in "rolling dormitories" to stay by the job which in most cases was not close to any towns.

Because the train construction went through the Native American lands, it was not uncommon to have a group of Cheyenne warriors bend rails and pull up tracks which had already been laid. When the destruction derailed a work train, the warriors looted and burned the train, and killed the crew.

After months of skirmishes known as "Red Cloud's War," the government suggested a treaty, but Native American leader Red Cloud would not condescend to meet until the military removed themselves from the Bozeman Trail. They agreed, and Red Cloud signed the Powder River Treaty, which guaranteed the Sioux their massive hunting ground in perpetuity. Red Cloud is considered the only native leader to have won a war against the United States. Amidst a crowd of dignitaries and workers, with the engines No. 119 and Jupiter practically touching noses, the Central Pacific and Union Pacific railroads joined together. On May 10, 1869 the two railroad lines met at Prometory Point, Utah. A crowd gathered and brass bands played. A railroad official raised a silver hammer and drove a gold spike into the last railroad tie. Telegraph operators transmitted to both coasts the blows of the hammer as it fell on a golden spike. The nation listened as west and east came together in undivided union. As telegraphs sent the message around the country, cannons blasted in New York, the Liberty Bell rang in Philadelphia and Chicago held a big parade. A trip between San Francisco and New York, which once took six months, now took people 10 days.

By 1880, the Pacific Railroad carried $50 million worth of freight annually. It served as artery for 200 million acres of settlement between the Pacific and Mississippi. The Plains Indians were scattered to reservations, and little over 1,000 buffalo remain of the millions that once populated the grasslands.

Researching Railroad Records

Learning about railroading ancestors requires looking into the history and geography of railroads. The Manuscript Collections of Virginia Tech are noteworthy, in particular the Manuscript Sources for Railroad History (http://spec.lib.vt.edu/railroad/rrintro.htm).

The images at the Library of Congress (www.loc.gov) and the National Archives and Records Administration (www.archives.gov), both have photographs and other materials relating to American railroads. The Library of Congress' American Memory has a collection of railroad maps online at http://memory.loc.gov/ammem/gmdhtml/rrhtml/rrhome.html.

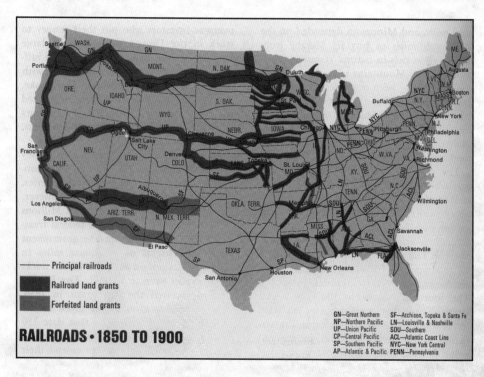

RAILROADS · 1850 TO 1900

Principal railroads
Railroad land grants
Forfeited land grants

GN—Great Northern   SF—Atchison, Topeka & Santa Fe
NP—Northern Pacific   LN—Louisville & Nashville
UP—Union Pacific   SOU—Southern
CP—Central Pacific   ACL—Atlantic Coast Line
SP—Southern Pacific   NYC—New York Central
AP—Atlantic & Pacific   PENN—Pennsylvania

George E Hodge

My great-grandfather, George Hodge grew up in Scotland. He became involved in working with the railroad while in Scotland. He later emigrated to Canada with his wife and children. Tempted by more lucrative work, George and his family moved to Missouri where he became the engineer of the railroad station there.

It is noted in family records that a "railroad mishap" at St. Joseph, Missouri in 1869 caused George to move his family to Utah in 1870. Family tradition says he was a conductor on one of the first trains through Utah which at the time the railroads had just connected east to west. He did not feel comfortable on trains again. Eventually he chose to move his family to Nebraska, still haunted by the mysterious train incident which happened years ago in Missouri. He lived out the rest of life farming in Nebraska. I still have not learned what the mishap was or why he was so haunted by working with trains. A new mystery to solve!

Did you know?

Once the railroads were connected there was no more use for the Pony Express, which until that time was the only way to get letters, and word across the country to keep people informed about what was going on in the country.

The spike in the photograph above is an actual golden spike used in the securing railroad tracks. Over the years, the spike has deteriorated to the point that it is flaking and falling apart. The two trains in the photograph are replicas of the actual trains that first met at Prometory Point, connecting east and west.

Orphan Train

Many poor immigrants coming to America in the late 19th and early 20th centuries discovered conditions in the new world were bleak. The immigrants found few jobs. Many found themselves unable to work or feed their children. Women died during childbirth or had illegitimate children for which they could not provide. Husbands died, leaving behind families. Some parents were alcoholics or committed crimes and put in prison. Many found their parents unable to care for them, and in desperation turned to the streets to sell newspapers, beg for food or steal. Moved by what he saw, Charles Loring Brace founded the Children's Aid Society of New York in 1853. He tried to establish schools to teach them skills. But attendance was poor and few learned a trade. No amount of orphanages could hold all the homeless children. He decided to send as many children as possible west to find homes with farm families. He sent notices to Midwest towns announcing the time and date a train-load of orphans would be arriving. The trains would leave New York City carrying the children and two adult agents from the society. As the train made its stops the children would be paraded in front of the crowd of onlookers. Some needed another farm hand. Others genuinely wanted to give a child a home. The train left a small part of its cargo at each stop until finally all the children found homes. The first train went to Michigan in 1854. The trains ran for 75 years with the last one pulling into Missouri in 1929. They had shipped more than 120,000 children ages 6 to 18.

Once on the train, the children were to break all ties to their past. The trains stopped at more than 45 states across the country as well as Canada and Mexico. Some children were adopted, some were indentured.

Later in life, without birth certificates, many children had legal problems as they grew older. These documents were required for marriage licenses, passports, social security cards, and driver's licenses.

Brace's group wasn't the only one sending orphans to the rural Midwest. Catholic Charities of New York also participated, perhaps because they saw Catholic children being placed in Protestant homes. In 1869 the Sisters of Mercy started the New York Foundling Hospital. Soon the Catholic group was sending its own "mercy trains" west.

Researching the Orphan Train

If you know your relative was in New York City between 1853–1929, was without parents, and ended up somewhere else in the country, you may want to look into the Orphan Train records. If you are fortunate enough to find a journal see if there is any reference to this phenomenon. You may want to check with other New York agencies as those listed below.

- Orphan Train
  Heritage Society of America
  4912 Trout Farm rd.
  Springdale AR. 72764

- National Genealogical Society
  4527 17th St. N.
  Arlington, VA 22207-2399
  Phone: (7030 525-0050
  www.genealogy.org/NGS

Other New York agencies that placed children:

- Children's Village (then known as the New York Juvenile Asylum)
- New York Foundling Hospital
- Graham-Windham Home for Children (then known as Orphan Asylum Society of the City of New York)
- New York Children's Aid Society

Thomas Hennessey

Family tradition puts my great grandfather in New York City in 1870, while his parents and siblings remained in their homeland of England.

The streets of New York at that time were filled with orphaned children due to parents out of work, in prison, or alcoholic and unable to care for their children. With so many orphaned children fending for themselves, I can only imagine that Thomas would have turned to stealing food, sleeping in abandoned buildings, and pandering to survive. I can understand that when the opportunity arose to escape these miserable conditions, Thomas jumped at it. Family tradition is that Thomas accepted the chance to go west on the Orphan Train.

The adventure led Thomas to Texas. I have found no record of a family taking him in but being almost 16 years old, I can see him starting a life on his own once the train reached the end of the trip. Rather than take an orphan back to New York, I believe he convinced them to let him find his way in the west rather than going back to the dangers and misery of the New York streets.

Tip:

If you find that a family member was involved in a certain historical event, but you are unable to secure any photographs, look for journal entries and photographs of people in similar situations. The picture of these boys on the train do not include my great grandfather, but gives an idea of what his experience may have been like. I was also able to understand his experience by reading the journals of others who were on the orphan train.

Don't be surprised to see your ancestor's name mentioned in someone else's journal. They spent significant time working and worshipping together and taking care of one another. Journal entries are a quality primary source because it was the actual person writing about his own experience at the time.

Ellis Island

The Statue of Liberty and Ellis Island are located in the New York Harbor. From 1892 to 1954, this depot processed the greatest tide of incoming humanity in the nation's history. Some twelve million people landed here. Today their descendants account for almost 40% of the country's population.

Opened on January 1, 1892, Ellis Island ushered in a new era of immigration with each newcomer's eligibility to land now determined by federal law. The government established a special bureau to process the record numbers that were arriving at the end of 19th century. Fleeing hardships such as poverty, religious persecution, or political unrest in their homelands, they journeyed to the United States in search of freedom and opportunity. More than 70% landed in New York, the country's largest port. First and second class passengers were processed on board ship, but third or steerage class were ferried to Ellis Island where they underwent medical and legal examinations.

Immigrants from all over the world funneled through Ellis Island: Italians, Irish, Polish, British, and German immigrants are a few. Many had to leave famished countries and endure months of weary travel, often separated from their families for years.

Researching Ellis Island Records

If your ancestors arrived in the United States between 1892–1924, the probability is extremely high that they passed through Ellis Island. Passenger manifest records were kept of the more than 22 million people who entered. Important information on each immigrant includes name, gender, age on arrival, marital status, ship name, port of origin, and last residence.

Ellis Island records are available online—www.ellisisland.org. If you know the name of your ancestor, where he left from, and the approximate departure date, you may find a photograph and information about the actual ship he was on, and a copy of the passenger list. You can order a certificate from the Ellis Island Organization with your relative's pertinent information typed on an attractive document.

Listed to the right are the facts I found online about Bob Hope's arrival to Ellis Island. The documents underneath are copies of the actual documents. I learned his mother and brothers' names as well as their ages and where they emigrated from. Of course, I needed to know that Bob Hope changed his name when he entered the country or I would not have known to look for Leslie Hape rather than Bob Hope. It was not uncommon for an immigrant to change his name when he arrived. He may have been emigrating for a reason and did not want to be found, he may want a name not so telling of the country he was from, or it may have just

been misunderstood and written differently on the records.

Information extracted from the documents below:

First Name: Leslie
Last Name: Hape
Ethnicity: England, English
Last Place of Residence:
Bristol, England
Date of Arrival: Mar 30, 1908
Age at Arrival: 2y
Gender: M
Marital Status: S
Ship of Travel: Philadelphia
Port of Departure: Southampton
Manifest Line Number: 0013

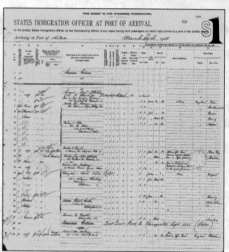

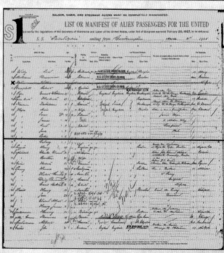

Bob Hope

Bob Hope was born "Leslie Townes Hope" in England in 1903. Bob recalls "my family came to America about 1908. My father, who arrived a year earlier, was a mason. I remember getting the vaccination for the steamship before we left and trying to run away from the doctor—he caught me. I don't remember the trip—I was only 5. We were in Ellis Island for a few hours. I remember standing with my mother and five brothers on the boat as it entered the New York Harbor and seeing the lights and the Statue of Liberty. I was wearing knickers and a cap, and it was cold. I remember looking at my mom when we passed inspection. We smiled and kissed and hugged each other because we had achieved this great rite of passage.

"When I made it in show business, I was performing down by the New York Harbor. I remember staring out over the water to Ellis Island and the Statue of Liberty and feeling grateful and saying to myself 'Thank you. Thanks for the memories.' Though in the movies, I have sung that song, when I hear it, I think of the day we arrived at Ellis Island."

The Philadelphia

Did you know?

The Statue of Liberty was a gift from the people of France to the people of the United States. It was the creation of Frederic Auguste Bartholdi, whose dream was to build a monument honoring the American spirit of freedom that has inspired the world. In 1874, scores of skilled French laborers began work on the statue. Bob's grandfather, James Hope was a stone mason. He participated in carving intricate parts for the construction of the Statue of Liberty in Paris.

69

Living Conditions

Newspapers have been called "the chronicle of everyday life," and they do indeed record the daily events at all levels. Look for news stories of the day that may have impacted your ancestors. Look at marriage announcements, obituaries, shipping news, weather reports, advertisements, and other news in the newspapers in or near the places they lived. Read through journals of your relatives and those contemporaries living by your relatives. This will give a better view into everyday life. Review almanacs of years surrounding your families' life in an area. Listen and interview older family members about what life was like for them during certain time periods in history. What was their chore responsibilities. Biggest fears. What was dinnertime like, bedtime, Sunday, school time? The most intriguing and exciting side of history, social history is how our ancestors lived their everyday lives. This can include everything from how people of the time behaved to how the events of the day affected them. As you research look at fashion, art, travel and communication, as well as politics and world events. Even new words or slang are often coined from the events of the day. Research the social restrictions and expectations for the different genders or ethnic groups of the time. What happened when someone deviated from the norm? In what sort of groupings did people like your relatives congregate?

Including everything that involved or affected your subject can be overwhelming. You may not wish to do much research. You can still add a splash of history to your heritage story. Consider including historical trivia about the period, which can be found quickly. For instance, as a background for your photos you may want to add the inventions of the day in either pictures or verbiage scattered about the page, or include popular social manners in journaling segments, or use pictures of the clothing fashions.

> To find where ancestors were living at a certain time refer to:
> - census
> - land and property records
> - biographies
> - gazateers
> - maps of the period
> - periodicals
> - city directory
> - taxation
> - voting records
> - church records
> - military records
>
> Land records show:
> - ownership
> - transfer of land
> - deeds
> - mortgages
> - brands
> - marks of ownership

Researching Living Conditions

When researching the lifestyles, clubs, and associates of your family members, your best resource would be the local county and state libraries where they were living. Valuable assets in local libraries are local histories and biographies. One of the most helpful resources is the librarian. Ask about what holdings are in the library and other resources in the community. Each city, county, and state is organized in a different manner and has different holdings.

From newspaper & periodical collections discover a wealth of information about your ancestors from many different kinds of newspapers, magazines, and periodicals. These types of sources can often supplement public records and provide information that is not recorded anywhere else. You can learn more about your ancestor's lives by placing them in the context of their daily lives.

Newspapers can contain a multitude of genealogical information- obituaries; notices of births, marriages, and deaths; legal notices; estate transactions; biographies, military, immigration.

Jack Cooper

Jack remembers spending the summer of 1941 with his grandparents who lived in an abandoned boxcar in Magma, Arizona.

"Our water was hauled in and Gran cooked on a wood burning stove. She did her cooking for the day early in the morning, trying to heat the house as little as possible. During the day, she sewed on a treadle machine and gathered wood.

"They had tamarack trees and a windmill which broke down one summer. Grandpa came home early and we took a 55 gallon barrel fitted on a skid. He hooked it to his saddle horn and we filled it with enough water for the summer.

"I slept on an iron-legged cot. Gran put each leg of the bed in a can of Kerosene so scorpions could not climb up them. At the end of the boxcar was a feed area for the horses with hay and grain. This brought in rats and varmints. The rats would run over my bed at night. We took a washtub full of water and covered it with hay. Then tied a string to the handle and put cheese in the center. In the morning, there would be two or three rats floating in the tub.

When the train passed by, they would throw me comic books and things to play with. I was seven or eight years old. I enjoyed every

minute. Gran would stand by the old wood cook stove with sweat pouring down her face. I can remember one of her favorite sayings 'I am sweating like a nigger at an election.'"

Did you know?

During the depression era people found shelter wherever they could. Whether it be a boxcar, under a bridge, or the back of a store, shelter was a premium for out of work families.

Chores

The days of old were filled with routine chores. The basic lifestyle changed over the years. Some of the chores and occupations no longer exist. We don't have to churn butter or survey the land through a gunsite. However, it is interesting to be reminded of how things were done "yesterday."

Chores were not limited to adults. Children were expected to work in the family business, on the farm, and around the house.

Keep a record of the chores and responsibilities you have now or had as a child. The chores done today will seem antiquated to future generations, just as the chores of grandparents seem so old fashioned.

Researching Household Duties

Where your family members lived and the type of work the father did, dictated the chores and responsibilities of the rest of the family members. If the father was a shop keeper all the children helped clean, stock and manage the shop. If the father owned a ranch, all the children had the chores of feeding, watering, and tending to the animals. Chores came before school. If it was a time of harvest or there was work to be done, school was not attended.

If a boy did not want to become a farmer when he grew up, he could become an apprentice to a craftsman and become a miller or blacksmith, etc.

The day of a pioneer child started with chores. Once completed, a short prayer was offered and a huge farm breakfast of oatmeal, eggs, bacon, milk, fresh bread and butter were served.

Chores of pioneer children:

- Clean the chicken coop
- Collect nuts and berries
- Empty slop jars each morning
- Feed/water animals
- Gather eggs
- Gather firewood or buffalo chips for cooking fires
- Get water from a stream
- Harvest ice
- Milk cows
- Pick fruit
- Pump water
- Scare off rabbits and squirrels from the crops with pots and pans
- Tend bees
- Trim wicks of kerosene lamps
- Weed garden

Chores children helped parents with:

- Plant and harvest crops
- Preserve fruits and vegetables from the garden
- Grind seed and sift it into flour

Pioneer boys' chores:

- Carve wood with a knife
- Chop and stack firewood
- Cut hay with a scythe
- Fish/hunt for small game
- Herd cattle
- Tame horses
- Tend crops
- Yoke oxen

Pioneer girls' chores:

- Card wool
- Churn butter/make cheese
- Collect feathers for bedding
- Cook food
- Do fancy stitching on samplers
- Make candles and soap
- Poke down the clothes in the wash pot of boiling water with a stick
- Roll out bread dough
- Sew, spin, and weave
- Wash dishes
- Watch smaller children
- Wring wet clothes

Everyone in the family learned to sew, including boys. They learned to put up hems, sew buttons, and were expected to knit their own suspenders.

When the children were traveling with a wagon:
- In areas where the trail was rough, walk ahead of the wagon and throw stones out of the way, clear brush, and put limbs and brush over muddy spots so that the wheels of the wagon would not sink in
- Help pack and unpack the bedding and cooking supplies from the wagon

Phoebe's Chores

When Phoebe Louisa Miller was a mother, in the early 1900s, she did not have a washing machine. She scrubbed the dirty clothes on a scrubbing board in a tub of water. Then boiled them in a copper boiler on the stove. People did not change clothes every day—maybe once a week in time for wash day.

Phoebe knitted the men's socks of grey wool yarn. When holes were worn in the socks she would mend them. She made all her children's clothes on a treadle sewing machine. She bought fleece wool from someone who had sheep, and picked strands of wool off of the fences where sheep walked. The wool was washed and dyed. The nit was pulled apart—it was called "picking" letting any remaining dirt, seeds, or twigs fall out onto newspaper. When done preparing the wool, she would card the wool into batts for quilts.

She pumped water by hand into a bucket and carried it into the house. She made a large noon time meal for her husband and anyone working in the field with him. Her stove had a big warming oven across the back top where she left leftover noontime dinner warm until her children got home from school.

Homesteading

To encourage people to advance the west, The Homestead Act of 1862 was signed into law by Abraham Lincoln after the secession of southern states. This Act turned over vast amounts of the public domain to private citizens. 270 million acres, or 10% of the area of the United States was claimed and settled under this act.

A homesteader had only to be the head of a household and at least 21 years of age to claim a 160 acre parcel of land. Settlers from all walks of life including newly arrived immigrants, farmers without land of their own from the East, single women and former slaves came to meet the challenge of "proving up" and keeping this "free land". Each homesteader had to live on the land, build a home, make improvements and farm for 5 years before they were eligible to "prove up".

The homestead entry papers are dated 1863-1908. A complete file includes a homestead application, the certificate of publication of intention to make a claim, the homestead final proof, and a final certificate authorizing the claimant to obtain a patent. The Homestead Final Proof Testimony, includes personal information such as the name, age, and post office of the claimant, a description of the tract, a description of the house, and the date when residence was established, the number and relationship of members in the family, evidence of citizenship, the nature of the crops, and number of acres under cultivation, and testimony of witnesses as to the truth of the claimant's statements.

When all requirements had been completed and the homesteader was ready, he found two neighbors or friends willing to vouch for the truth of his or her statements about the land's improvements and sign the "proof" document.

After successful completion of this final form, the homesteader received the patent for the land, signed with the name of the current President of the United States. This paper was often proudly displayed on a cabin wall.

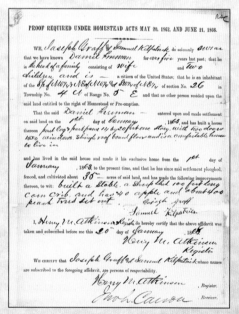

Patent for the Land

Application

Final Proof

Hennessey Homestead

In 1887, Thomas Hennessey homesteaded some land in Coke County Texas. The area was chiefly stock range, but there were a few farms producing peanuts, watermelon, cotton, and fruit. It was not a fertile country and there was little rainfall. This 5'8" man weighing no more than 135 pounds, found it difficult to live in the primitive, frontier of Texas. This was very different from the lifestyle he grew up with in London.

Thomas, as many ranchers of the time, became discouraged and became an alcoholic. Eventually he lost the deed to the homestead. My grandmother, Matilda Jane, worked and begged to get the land back. After succeeding and 28 years of marriage, she divorced Thomas and was given custody of their remaining six minor children. She lived out the rest of her life on the homestead with some help from her sons.

Adams' Oilfield

Homesteaders did not always succeed in gaining ownership of land. My great-grandfather Ichabod Adams immigrated from England. Enticed by the promise of free land to homesteaders, he took his family west.

Unfortunately Ichabod was not prepared to be a rancher and was unfamiliar with the type of land offered in Texas.

As Ichabod worked the land, he could get nothing to grow. He treated the crops and land as he had been taught in England but the soil and climate was much different. His crops continued to fail. Eventually, he lost the homesteaded land to debt. He and his wife died as paupers of malnutrition. In later years, it was discovered that the land would not produce crops because it was on a large oil deposit. It became one of the richest oil fields in Texas.

Tip:
If your relatives were homesteaders, find the land records to learn where the land was located. Secure a map true to the time period and plot where the family homesteaded. Look in early photographs of the family in hopes of seeing what the land looked like at the time. Visit the homesteaded land. Record the coordinates so someone could find it today. What does it look like today? What has become of the land? Is it still in the possession of a family member?

Relationships

Medieval Times

In the 16th century, marriages were usually arranged, especially among the upper classes where dynastic fortunes were at stake. The children of the upper classes typically married young, as dynastic obligations were one of their social duties. The lower classes did not marry until a man had either acquired a piece of land to work or was established in a trade, while a woman and her family needed to save for her dowry.

Marriage was primarily an economic and business relationship, not a sentimental one, and was therefore carefully contracted like any business deal.

Death in childbirth was common enough that a man went through several wives.

Many women were treated like possessions. The men were in charge and the women were their servants. Some women followed along—some did not. The couples' understanding and compliance of what the relationship should be often determined how the couple got along.

Researching Relationships

- Family journal
- History books—learn what types of relationships were expected for the time period

William & Mary Shurtliff

My great grandfather, William Shurtliff graduated from Harvard College in 1707. In 1732, he was chosen to succeed the Reverend John Emerson, deceased. He was the first pastor after the Old South Church was erected there.

My great grandmother Mary refused to be a servant to William.

The utter disrespect with which she had for her husband and his position was outrageous at a time in New England when clerical dignity was at its highest sensitive point. She let his ruffles go unstarched, scandalized him by wearing frivolous colors, left him to cook his own dinner, and locked him in his study while he was praying before a service. This type of behavior was appalling for the time period.

Native Americans

When the immigrants started settling parts of the west, they needed to learn to live with the Native American ways. Some native tribes were hostile, some were domicile, depending on their previous experience with the immigrants.

Indians have lived in America for thousands of years. They introduced agriculture. They grew maize, squash, beans, and cotton, partly with the use of irrigation systems. Three Indian tribes—the Anasazi, Mogollon, and Hohokam—built the earliest settlements.

Many Native Americans live today much as their ancestors did.

Tribes are grouped by the language they speak. The Native Americans greatly influenced the history of America. Many cities, counties, mountains, and so on have Native American names.

As miners and farmers moved west and south, Native Americans resisted. Several times the Native Americans tried to drive out the Spaniards, but the Spanish soldiers regained any territory they lost.

As the Civil War intensified, the cavalry withdrew the troops who had guarded against the Apaches. The Native Americans attacked the isolated, unprotected homesteads. The 25 years after the Civil War brought both Indian wars and progress.

In 1830, the Indian Removal Act was passed, giving the President the power to move the natives from American settlements. After 1871, the tribes were no longer considered separate governments. This meant the government could take action concerning the natives without negotiating treaties. More and more Native Americans were relocated to reservations. Today Indian Nations are sovereign governments, recognized in the Constitution and hundreds of treaties. The history of these original inhabitants encompasses a broad range of cultures and experiences.

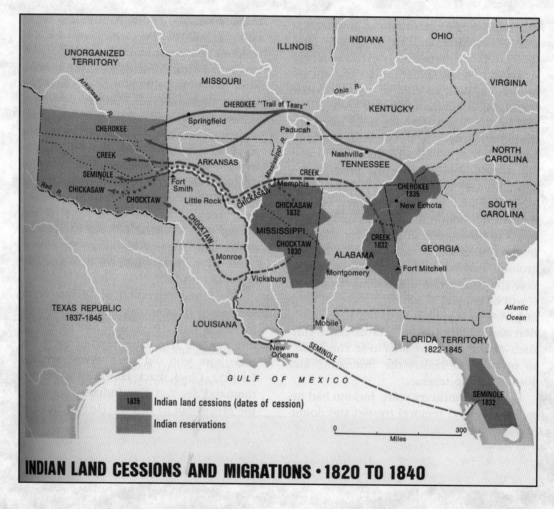

INDIAN LAND CESSIONS AND MIGRATIONS · 1820 TO 1840

Lillie Hennessey

My grandmother Lillie lived near the Navajo reservation in Arizona in 1914. The family home was on the main trail from Holbrook to Keams Canyon. Native Americans passed by her home on their travels every day. Sometimes as many as 10 wagons at a time. They always stopped at her home because it was the only watering hole on the route.

One day while her husband Ed was away from the ranch, one of the Native Americans came over to the house and asked Lillie for something to eat. She went into the kitchen to slice some bread for a sandwich when she heard the screen door open. The Native American had slipped in and sat down at the table. Lillie had a big butcher knife in her hand and shook it at the man stating, "I will feed you, but you are not welcome in my home." He scurried outside and waited on the step for his lunch.

This was typical behavior in the relationship between the Native Americans and the white settlers in Arizona at that time period.

In the 1920s, ED AND LILLIE HENNESSEY lived on a ranch 25 miles north of Holbrook, Arizona. This was on the main trail from Holbrook to Keams Canyon on the NAVAJO RESERVATION Indians passed by the ranch every day. They stopped at the ranch because it was the only water on the route. It was not uncommon for them to knock on the door for food. One time an Indian asked for lunch. Lillie went into the kitchen and was slicing bread when she heard the screen door open. The Indian slipped in and sat down at the table. Lillie had a big BUTCHER KNIFE in her hand and shook it at him. He got out quickly and waited for his lunch on the porch. The white man and the Navajos were not friends. They tolerated one another.

Did you know?

In 1862, Congress passed an act giving free land to anyone who moved to the Great Plains. The Native Americans who lived on the plains were promised money for their land. But the Union spent this money on the Civil War instead. Soon, wars started between settlers and Native Americans.

Did you know?

The Plains Indians developed their way of life around the buffalo. They used the buffalo in 52 different ways for food, supplies, war and hunting implements. The hooves were boiled for glue. The hump back was used to make shields, the hides were used to make tepees. The buffalo was the most important natural resource to the Plains Indians. After settlers and the railroad buffalos became nearly extinct.

Neighbors

Despite the distance between homes, homesteading families turned to one another for support and companionship, creating networks of community both formal and informal. Though homesteaders were self-sufficient in many ways, they relied on their neighbors during the settling-in period and during the inevitable hard times.

You may notice by reviewing census records that your ancestors' neighbors tend to be the same people even after they moved. It was not uncommon for neighbors to travel as a group. They usually shared the same religious and ethnic values. They were in the same line of work such as farming or mining. When family members migrated together they were able to help each other.

When reviewing vital documents it would not be uncommon to have a neighbor sign as a witness to a baptism or marriage.

When someone was ill, died, or needed a barn built, the neighbor relationship was especially important. Children may even be named after neighbors or even raised by them. When living in rural areas, the next door neighbor, though miles away, may be the only contact a family would have for weeks or even months.

In the above census my great grandparents William and Nancy Martin are shown living next door to N. M. Martin. I currently do not know this neighbor. However, since they have the same last name and live next door to one another, they may be related. This is a clue for further research.

Researching my Family's Neighbors

Find your ancestors' neighbors by checking census records and seeing who is listed next door. When reading journal entries or old letters look for any reference or mention of those living nearby. Also review documents where additional signatures were required. Neighbors and friends were commonly used as references and signed one another's documents.

Phoebe Miller

My great grandparents George and Phoebe Miller married in 1902. They purchased 512 acres of land in Star Valley Wyoming, with a small frame house and a few sheds for livestock. The work on the ranch was demanding and the winters were severe. The couple worked the land and raised several children.

The only time Phoebe went into town or visited with others was on Sunday when the family went into town for church. Her closest neighbor was a mile away. Though they had little in common personally, the neighbor and Phoebe canned fruit together, shared surplus crops, helped one another with sick children, helped with spring cleaning duties, and shared winter food storages.

During the great influenza epidemic in 1918, whole families were in bed at once, several people in the valley died. Not only did the sick require help, but the livestock needed to be fed and milked. Phoebe worked tirelessly caring for other families. After the worse of it passed Phoebe became terrible sick from being so run down and infected by so many other families. It was her "close" neighbor who came to take care of her and her children and farm duties.

Did you know?

It was common to name a child after a favorite neighbor. When checking census records, compare children names with those of the neighbors. If names match, research as to why this neighbor was so special to your family. You may find it to even be a distant relative.

Following is a quote from a homesteader in the 18th century:
"I have just as good neighbors as I ever had any where. I was never in a neighborhood where all was as near on equality as they are here.... Everyone is on his own and doing the best he can."

Old Country Traditions

Immigration plays a big role in the evolution of many traditions. Traditions are, in a sense, transplanted to the United States due to immigration. The traditions are sometimes the only thing the immigrants have to remind them of home. From St. Patrick's Day to Christmas, ethnic cultural traditions have found a broad appeal. Some traditions, superstitions, and celebrations were embraced, while some were not. Some still are cherished today. The responsibility for the passing on of family stories and traditions lies not with the older generation to tell, but with the younger generation to ask. This could include celebration traditions, passing down of a name, or even father choosing mates for his daughters.

Read historical books on traditions and how they originated or where they were practiced. Then look into your own family to see if they were followed or changed a bit or ignored when they came to America. The best place to research is through oral interviews and journals of family members.

If you are struggling with trying to find where your family came from, learn what some of their traditions were and which ones they observed and held in high regard. Then find what countries or even parts within a country followed those same traditions.

Traditions celebrated by various countries include:

- Maypole dancing
- Arranged marriages
- Women covering their faces
- Using a matchmaker
- Circumcision
- Smorgasbord
- Germans invented the American weekend with Sunday recreation and Sunday outings.
- The Christmas tree was brought over to the United States by German immigrants.
- Santa Claus has its roots in the drawings of a German-born immigrant.
- The Easter egg hunt is a custom enjoyed by German children.

Researching Family Traditions

Family tradition information will only come from family members. Ask living relatives about traditions centering around holidays, celebrations, and important events. After interviewing relatives, review the follow sources to find more about typical family traditions of the day.

which has become an integral holiday tradition within American culture.

- Immigrant families depended on their children. They relied on the speed with which children learned English, as well as their earning capabilities.
- Rural and urban children were employed in various sectors of the economy, from side jobs like selling newspapers or shining shoes to working in textile mills and factories. In cities throughout Wisconsin, immigrant children could be found working in the brewing and textile industries, as well as in workshops, bakeries, and butcher shops which were often family owned.

Bagpiper

Being of Scottish descent, my family traditionally has had a single bagpiper play at the graveside during a family member's burial. The sound of the pipes releases the spirit. Once the spirit is gone, the piper plays a tune such as "Scotland the Brave" as he marches away over a nearby hill. Though this action shows that the piper has done his job and the spirit has moved on, it also reminds us that our loved one has gone but his song can be heard in the distance until we meet again.

Historically for a Scottish person, the war-pipes were far more than a musical instrument. They drove men into a killing rage and put fear in the hearts of their enemies. They were used to remember their fallen comrades and express grief at their loss; and after a battle, the joy of their living. Today, the bagpipes tell us of our history, and remind us of the brave deeds of the warriors that came before us. The sound of the pipes is the music of our strongest emotions.

My family has a single bagpiper play at the graveside of a family member's funeral. This tradition came from our native land Scotland. Traditionally, the sound of the pipes release the spirit.

Once the spirit is gone, the piper plays a tune such as "Scotland the Brave" as he marches away over a nearby hill in the cemetery. This represents that the piper has done his job and the spirit has moved on. This act also reminds us that our loved one has gone but their song can be heard in the distance until we meet again.

Tip:
Your heritage scrapbook will be ever evolving. As family members enjoy your work, they may share additional information about the events you have scrapbooked. Be receptive to this information.

If one of your family's traditions was having a bagpiper play at a family graveside services, encourage family members to respond to how bagpipes make them feel. What does this tradition mean to you and other family members? Continue to add information to your layout to make it more complete and meaningful.

83

Superstitions

Family stories, legends, and superstition sometimes have an effect on what your ancestors did or the decisions they made. Some are still followed today without even knowing the origin or the meaning.

Superstitions believed by various countries include:

• Amber beads, worn as a necklace, can protect against illness or cure colds.

• To protect yourself from witches, wear a blue bead.

• Placing a bed facing north and south brings misfortune.

• If a bee enters your home, it's a sign that you will soon have a visitor. If you kill the bee, you will have bad luck, or the visitor will be unpleasant.

• A swarm of bees settling on a roof is an omen that the house will burn down.

• The sound of bells drives away demons because they're afraid of the loud noise.

• The Blarney Stone is a stone set in the wall of the Blarney Castle tower in the Irish village of Blarney. Kissing the stone brings the kisser the gift of persuasive eloquence.

• A bird in the house is a sign of a death.

• To prevent an unwelcome guest from returning, sweep out the room they stayed in immediately after they leave.

• If a candle lighted as part of a ceremony blows out, it is a sign that evil spirits are nearby.

• Cats near a baby "sucks the breath" of the child.

• A cat onboard a ship brings good luck.

• Evil spirits can't harm you when you stand inside a circle.

• If a clock which has not been working suddenly chimes, there will be a death in the family.

• It is unlucky to see your face in a mirror by candlelight.

• Throw back the first fish you catch and you'll be lucky the whole day fishing.

• Any ship that sails on Friday will have bad luck.

• Never start to make a garment on Friday unless you can finish it the same day.

• A horseshoe, hung above the doorway, will bring good luck to a home. In most of Europe protective horseshoes are placed in a downward facing position, but in some parts of Ireland and Britain people believe that the shoes must be turned upward or "the luck will run out."

• Ivy growing on a house protects the inhabitants from evil.

• A knife placed under the bed during childbirth eases labor pain.

• Don't knit a pair of socks for your boyfriend or he'll walk away from you.

• It's bad luck to leave a house through a different door than the one used to come into it.

• A mirror should be covered during a thunderstorm because it attracts lightening.

• Mistletoe in the house protects it from thunder and lightning. It also cures many diseases, is an antidote to poison and brings good luck and fertility.

• An onion cut in half and placed under the bed of a sick person will draw off fever and poisons.

• It is bad luck to see an owl in the sunlight.

• A red ribbon should be placed on a child who has been sick to keep the illness from returning.

• If you leave a rocking chair rocking when empty, it invites evil spirits to come into your house to sit in the rocking chair.

• If you drop scissors, it means your lover is being unfaithful.

• The devil can enter your body when you sneeze. Having someone say, "God bless you," drives the devil away.

• A bride's veil protects her from evil spirits who are jealous of happy people.

Joseph & Rebecca Argyle

When Joseph Argyle was 14 years old, he was bound by his father as an apprentice to Thomas Dudley of Market Bosworth, England until he was 21. Dudley provided Joseph with room and board while he trained in the trade of tin plate work.

After 7 years, Joseph found work in Lemington making gas meters. The last night of October in 1840 Joseph needed lodging enroute to his new job. He found an inn owned by William and Rebecca Finch.

Meanwhile, the innkeeper's daughter, Jane returned home late from a Halloween party. She and a friend decided to try an old superstition. They were to blindfold themselves and go to bed backwards. The first man they saw after going to bed would be their future husband. Jane blindfolded herself, backed to her bed, and reached for her pillow. Her hand rested on a mass of hair. Her scream woke up Joseph who had gone to bed in the wrong room.

Joseph and Jane began courting and married two months later on 24 Dec 1840. During their 50 years of marriage they had 12 children.

Wars

Each war in American history has generated military records that are valuable in genealogical research. Regardless of rank from private to general, all servicemen have records.

Military records provide valuable information while placing your relative in the wars. When a family member is found in an event such as a war, history has a new meaning, and the sacrifices that were made for us by our ancestors strike a chord deep within us.

Researching War Records

Refer to as many war records are possible. Each offers something unique. Depending on the war and where their allegiance was will have some bearing on what information was preserved. Regardless of the war consider the following sources which could be helpful in any war situation.

- Journals
- National archives
- Service records
- Unit histories
- Census
- Military record
- Hometown newspapers
- Obituaries
- Probate
- Town records
- Vital records
- Tombstones

Most records in existence relating to early wars, are in the National Archives in Washington, D.C. Paper copies of records can be ordered by mail using one NATF Form 80 for each soldier and each type of file. You can obtain the Form 80 by providing your name and mailing address to inquire@nara.gov. Be certain to specify "Form 80" and the number of forms you need.

The military file will have the enlistment form and service record while the pension file contains family and health information.

Pension files are usually filled with testimonials from fellow comrades or commanders who served with the veteran. Often there is additional testimonies or affidavits submitted by family members or doctors during the period after the veteran was discharged from service. Pensions could be claimed by widows or other survivors.

Tombstone inscriptions and cemetery markers may provide the unit in which the deceased served. Once you know your relatives regiment, locate information about the unit. This additional information will give you a greater sense of the role that your ancestor played in history. Regimental histories detail the duties of particular groups of men within the unit as well as the hardships endured and the triumphs enjoyed by the entire unit. Many contain rather complete listings of all the skirmishes, battles, and other engagements in which the unit participated.

Soldiers' diaries provide detail about military engagements and the people involved. Sometimes lists of soldiers captured, encountered, and reprimanded can be found. Soldiers' letters home may contain names of other individuals fighting with him as well as heartfelt stories of the trials of war. Such letters may be found in local city and county archives as well as at a soldier's home state archives. If you are unable to find personal journal from your family member, referring to other soldiers thoughts will shed some light on what your soldier's experience was like.

Publications of various military and patriotic organizations are a good source. The Confederate Veteran, the Daughters of the American Revolution Magazine, and Southern Magazine published by the United Daughters of the Confederacy are a few such publications. These may provide copies of actual records, indexes of major collections of military data, lists of recently published regimental histories, and names of individuals to contact for special assistance.

Because communities had so much pride in the local boys at war you can find a wealth of information in local newspapers as well as town and area publications. If you know the community from which an ancestor entered the service, returned after service, or died, the local history material available will be invaluable.

Tip:
Provide a brief history of a relative's military career along with any copies of service records and photos, metals, citations, or other military memorabilia you have found. Research and include tidbits of info from the regimental or unit histories.

Service records include:

Company musters
Rolls
Rosters
Enlistments
Discharge records
Discharge lists
Prisoner of war records
Records of burials
Oaths of allegiance

Military records to check:

Pension records
Bounty land warrants
Claims records
General military histories
Unit/regimental histories

Wars

King William's War 1689-1697
Queen Anne's War 1702-1713
King George's War 1744-1748
French/Indian War 1754-1763
Revolutionary War 1775-1783
War of 1812 1812-1815
Mexican/American War
    1846-1848
Civil War 1861-1865
Spanish/American War 1898
Philippine Insurrection
    1899-1902
World War I 1917-1918
World War II 1941-1945
Korean War 1950-1953
Vietnam War 1961-1975

Did you know?

Dwight D. Eisenhower's prayer was published in 1943. "Almighty God, we are about to be committed to a task from which some of us will not return. We go willingly to this hazardous adventure because we believe that those concepts of human dignity, rights and justice that Your Son expounded to the world, and which are respected in the government of our beloved country, are in peril of extinction from the earth. We are ready to sacrifice ourselves for our country and our God. We do not ask, individually, for our safe return. But we earnestly pray that You will help each of us to do his full duty. Permit none of us to fail a comrade in the fight. Above all, sustain us in our conviction in the justice and righteousness of our cause so that we may rise above all terror of the enemy and come to You, if called, in the humble pride of the good soldier and in the certainty of Your infinite mercy. Amen.

Revolutionary War

In the mid 1700s, the colonies in North America were becoming increasingly troublesome for the British. Though they offered important trade and territorial possibilities, they were expensive to defend and increasingly headstrong. In 1763, Britain issued a decree limiting western expansion in North America. This added to the tensions concerning regulation to commerce and taxation. The conflict increased as Britain tried to assert its control over the colonies, and the colonies sought to run their own affairs.

Major events which led to independence:

1764—The Currency Act
1765—The Sugar Act
1766—The Townshend Act
1770—The Boston Massacre
1773—The British Tea Act
1773—The Boston Tea Party
1774—The Intolerable Acts
1774—1st Continental Congress
1775—Lexington and Concord
1775—2nd Continental Congress
1775—The Battle of Bunker Hill
1776—Declaration of Independence
1777—Articles of Confederation
1777—Valley Forge
1787—Constitution of the U.S.
1789—George Washington elected President

Researching Revolutionary War Records

Many service records relating to the Revolutionary War were destroyed when the British burned Washington during the War of 1812. Service and pension files were first created as a result of the Revolutionary War (1775-1784) Pension records relating to service in the Revolutionary War were created under various Congressional acts beginning in 1776 and continuing into the 20th century.

The pension application files relating to claims for service between the end of the Revolution 11 Apr 1783 and the beginning of the Civil War 4 Mar 1861. These files are in the National Archives in Washington D.C. An alphabetical name index has been reproduced on seven rolls of microfilm and is available at the Genealogical Library or through a local Genealogical Library.

Documents relating to a soldier, his widow, or his children have been combined in a single packet or file in the National Archives and are available to the genealogist. The files have also been microfilmed and are available through the Genealogical Library in Salt Lake City. The microfilm is alphabetically arranged by the name of the soldier and a published index also exists.

Membership records of hereditary societies and patriotic organizations have long been regarded as excellent genealogical sources. Most require a formal application for membership, usually requiring a family connection to some colonial group or citizen. Such organizations may include the Sons of the American Revolution or Daughters of the American Revolution.

The Daughters of the American Revolution has original materials as well as a large collection of family histories and cemetery records collected from local chapters around the country. The collection covers local history, including town, state, county, and church materials. Genealogies, biographies, and vital records are also available.

Tip:
If no family photographs are available of an historical event such as of the Revolutionary War, find clip art or renderings that relate to the time period, occupation, or the social aspect. Look through old history books, encyclopedias, and magazines for the colors, moods, and images that would most accurately portray the event.

Sylvester Adams

Revolutionary War service is claimed for my great grandfather Sylvester, but there seems to be no definite proof of his service. With further research, I found two different soldiers with the name Sylvester Adams but neither were my great grandfather. Instead I learned that the land Sylvester took up in Tennessee was not his own bounty land, but the assignee of Philip Dean who served from North Carolina. It was a common practice for a soldier to sell his bounty land warrant to someone else, which was evident in this case.

On Dec 1, 1808 Sylvester received the grant from Philip Dean containing 100 acres lying in Dickson County. The deed was recorded in 1810 and by then the land was in newly formed Humphreys County. This land later became known as the Adams Farm where both Sylvester and his wife Rebecca both lived out their lives and were buried. For the next 100 years Adams relatives were buried on this land in unmarked graves. The little cemetery was eventually plowed under in 1940.

Do not assume anything. Continue to look through records to be certain the facts gathered are accurate to your deduction.

Revolutionary War service is claimed for Sylvester Adams, but there seems to be no proof of his service. On the contrary, the land he settled in Tennessee was not his own bounty land, but was assigned to Philip Dean who served in the war from North Carolina.

It was a common practice for a soldier to sell his bounty land warrant to someone else, which was evident in this case.

On Dec 1, 1808 Sylvester received a grant from Philip Dean for 100 acres in Dickson County, Tennessee. The deed was recorded in 1810 and by then the land was in newly formed Humphreys County.

This land became known as the Adams Farm where both Sylvester and his wife Rebecca both died and were buried.

For the following 100 years, Adams relatives were buried on this land in unmarked graves. The little cemetery was plowed under in 1940.

Did you know?

In colonial times, women defended their homes and families against Indian attacks and later supported the American soldiers battling the British, first in the Revolutionary War and later in the War of 1812. They provided foodstuffs, livestock, clothing, and many other things to support their troops.

Tip:
As you research it would be an interesting project to see if any of your relatives fought against each other being from two different countries at the time.

Civil War

When Lincoln became president, many southerners believed Lincoln's election would mean abolition and rebellion by slaves.

In the south, government leaders owned large plantations. They grew tobacco, cotton, and sugar, which they sold to market. They plantations depended on slaves to plant and pick their crops.

In the north, most government leaders were involved in factories and businesses. They could manage their affairs without slaves. So many northerners were willing to support abolitionists who wanted to make slavery illegal.

Seven states eventually withdrew from the Union. They drafted their own constitution for their new alliance—the Confederate States of America and called on other slave states to join them.

Soon a battle began in which countrymen fought against each other, North against South, brother against brother, father against son. The war split many families apart. A son may have fought for the North while his father fought for the South.

Women assumed the roles of men by working the family farms and providing for their families while their husbands and sons were at war. Sometimes the women did this against almost unbearable odds, risking their lives and the lives of their children.

Southern households found it difficult to feed their families. Women left on the plantations struggled with the large workload.

Wives left on small farms in rural South were especially hard hit without the help of slaves or male family members. Families were stripped of husbands, sons, mules, tools, and firearms.

Researching the Union Soldiers Records

The Federation of Genealogical Societies (FGS) is involved in the Civil War Soldiers and Sailors System. The FSG has combined the resources of volunteers nationwide to help the National Park Service create a database, which is available to visitors at some of the park service's Civil War sites.

As with other war records, Civil War information can be found online through FamilySearch.org, Ancestry.com or www.fgs.org.

Ulysses S. Grant Civil War Pension Record

Some women, on both sides of the Civil War, disguised themselves as men so they could participate in the fighting. Above is a picture of Mary Tippee in her uniform. She went through the war registered under the name of Charles Fuller.

Abraham Lincoln

President Lincoln was named after his grandfather Abraham Lincoln who lived in the Virginia Colony and fought in the Revolutionary War.

Grandfather Abraham was outgoing and in 1782 traveled to Kentucky with his friend Daniel Boone. President Lincoln respected his ancestors and had a deep commitment for the freedom of his namesake.

Did you know?

• Three of Mary Todd Lincoln's brothers died in the Civil War fighting for the South.

• Because men had been at war for two planting seasons, harvests across the country were poor and grain storehouses were nearly empty.

• In gratitude of freedom after the Civil War, President Lincoln set aside the last Thursday in November as a national day of Thanksgiving beginning in 1863.

• In 1862, Walt Whitman went to a field hospital to care for his wounded brother. He then moved to Washington D.C. where he got a job as a government clerk and spent his spare time caring for wounded soldiers.

• More than 3000 women served as nurses during the war. One such woman was Louisa May Alcott who spent time in Washington hospitals before returning to Concord to write her first book, "Hospital Sketches" then "Little Women."

Researching Confederate Soldiers Records

Most Confederate veteran's records are not in the National Archives, but are located in the state from which they served as pensions for them were granted by state governments, not federal.

Many Confederate records relating to hospitals, medical purveyors, medical directors, and other "Records of the Medical Department, Confederate War Department 1861–65" (NARA Record Group 109.8) are held by NARA in their Record Group 109. For a complete listing, visit the NARA website (www.archives.gov).

Confederate women volunteered their time and service to assisting in hospitals and Confederate soldiers' homes following the Civil War, and in cleaning and maintaining the gravesites of the Confederate dead.

The United Daughters of the Confederacy (UDC) is an outgrowth of many local memorial, monument, and Confederate home associations and auxiliaries to camps of United Confederate Veterans (UCV) that were organized after the War.

Following the Civil War, an organization was founded called the United Confederate Veterans (UCV) and posts were formed in many places in the South to preserve the history and legacy of the South and the veterans. The heir to the UCV heritage is the Sons of the Confederacy (SCV), founded in Richmond, Virginia, in 1896. The organization is open to all male descendants of any veteran who served in the Confederate armed forces. The SCV actively promotes the registration of Confederate graves, genealogical research, and memorial awards. You can learn more about the SCV at www.scv.org.

Between 1893 and 1932, the Confederate Veteran magazine was published. Each issue was filled with information, stories, obituaries, and recollections of the Confederate armed forces during the Civil War. Broadfoot Publishing Company (www.broadfootpublishing.com) reprinted all the issues of the Confederate Veteran, and these can be found in many larger libraries' genealogical and local history collections.

War of 1812 Resources

- Confederate soldiers' homes
- United Daughters of the Confederacy
- Sons of the Confederacy
- Confederate Veteran magazine
- Ancestry.com's Family and Local Histories Collection contains a number of memoirs, diaries, journals, and published Confederate rosters of the era.

Ichabod & Ann Hooper Adams

Ichabod Adams was considered a successful man with large land holdings and numerous slaves. His personal property was documented as $12,000 on the 1860 US census. These possessions were mostly slaves. However in an interesting document I found—all the property was really owned by his wife Ann.

A document filed in August, 1850 reads… "Ann C. C. Hooper wife of Ichabod Adams…filed with the clerk of the district court for the parish and state aforesaid a petition in the words and figures following to wit: (the names and descriptions of 15 slaves and given)…Petitioner further represents that the slaves are her property and belong to her in her own right. That said slaves are now administered by her husband Ichabod Adams. Petitioner further represents that her husband is in debt and embarrassed circumstances and that she fears she may lose her property…Petitioner further represents that a separation of property and a dissolution of the community of acquits and gains will be her separate property." Though Ann eventually gained ownership of her property, all was lost when the slaves were freed at the end of the Civil War.

Did you know?

A few slave owners were black themselves: a small percentage of free blacks owned slaves, in some cases essentially as a fiction so that they could protect family members, but more often to profit, like other slaveholders, from free labor. In addition to performing fieldwork, slaves served as house servants, nurses, midwives, carpenters, blacksmiths, drivers, preachers, gardeners, and handymen.

Owners relied heavily on children, the elderly, and the infirm for "nonproductive" work—such as house service.

War of 1812

The War of 1812 was fought between the United States and Great Britain. The war lasted for over two years, and while it ended much like it started; in stalemate; it was in fact a war that confirmed American Independence.

The offensive actions of the United States failed in every attempt to capture Canada.

On the other hand, the British army was successfully stopped when it attempted to capture Baltimore and New Orleans. There were a number of American naval victories in which American vessels proved themselves superior to similarly sized British vessels.

The main land fighting of the war occurred along the Canadian border, in the Chesapeake Bay region, and along the Gulf of Mexico; some action also took place at sea.

From the end of the American Revolution in 1783, the United States had been irritated by the failure of the British to withdraw from American territory along the Great Lakes; their backing of the Indians on America's frontiers; and their unwillingness to sign commercial agreements.

American resentment grew during the French Revolutionary Wars (1792-1802) and the Napoleonic Wars (1803-15), in which Britain and France were the main combatants.

The embargo failed to change British and French policies but devastated New England shipping.

Failing in peaceful efforts and facing an economic depression, some Americans began to argue for a declaration of war to redeem the national honor. The Congress that was elected in 1810 and met in November 1811 included a group known as the War Hawks who demanded war against Great Britain. Napoleon's announcement in 1810 of the revocation of his decrees was followed by British refusals to repeal their orders, and pressures for war increased.

On June 18, 1812, President James Madison signed a declaration of war. Unknown to the Americans, Britain had finally, two days earlier, announced that it would revoke its orders.

U.S. forces were not ready for war, and American hopes of conquering Canada collapsed in the campaigns of 1812 and 1813. America won a series of single-ship engagements with British frigates, and American privateers continually harried British shipping. Meanwhile, the British gradually tightened a blockade around America's coasts, ruining American trade, threatening American finances, and exposing the entire coastline to British attack.

The Treaty of Ghent, which ended the War of 1812 but resolved none of the issues that started it, had been signed in Europe weeks before the action on the Chalmette Plantation.

The soldiers' children were conditioned to hate the English and the children of the Orleans troops followed their example. They would appoint times and places to meet the English boys for battle and often two to one.

Researching War of 1812 Records

War of 1812 pension records along with Indian Wars Pension Records and Mexican War Pension Records are all available in the National Archives.

Each record includes the soldier's name, company, rank at time of induction, rank at time of discharge, and other helpful information. It provides the names of nearly 600,000 men. Each volunteer soldier has one Compiled Military Service Record (CMSR) for each regiment in which he served. The CMSR contains basic information about the soldier's military career, and it is the first source the researcher should consult.

CMSR records include:
- enlistment papers
- date of enlistment
- date of discharge
- attendance
- birth place if foreign born
- hospitalization for injury/illness
- papers relating to capture and release as a prisoner of war
- wounds received during battle
- amount of bounty paid him

John Christopher Kartchner

When the War of 1812 broke out, my 4th great grandfather, John Christopher Kartchner, volunteered to fight. He went by ship to Mobile, then to New Orleans under General Jackson's command. In his absence his wife Prudence had a baby. On John's arrival home he greatly rejoiced over his little "warrior" which became the baby's nickname.

In 1820, John and Prudence had my 3rd great grandfather, William Decatur. He was named William after Prudence's grandfather William Walton (who signed the Declaration of Independence) and Decatur after John's commanding officer from the War of 1812, Stephen Decatur. William knew the importance of his namesake meaning which inspired him throughout his life.

Did you know?

Events that transpired during the war inspired Francis Scott Key, an American lawyer detained on a British ship, to write the Star-Spangled Banner while he watched the attack on Fort McHenry.

Did you know?

Six of the soldiers's wives were allowed in camp for every 100 soldiers. They were chosen by lottery.

The women were employed as seamstresses, nurse maids, laundry maids, and scullery maids. It is said that the women were given the hard jobs and the men looked after the dangerous jobs. The women also cooked and cleaned for their own families, the life was very hard and the women were very much respected by the men.

If a woman's husband was killed or died she had 3–6 months to grieve and then she had to remarry or leave the camp, most remarried for the security. There are at least 2 reports of women who married 4 times in 5 months because their husbands died.

95

World War I

On 6 April 1917, the United States declared war on Germany and officially entered World War I. Six weeks later, every male living within the United States between the ages of eighteen and forty-five was required to register for the draft.

In large cities, it was essential to have maps produced that indicated the boundaries of the individual draft boards. Sometimes these maps and corresponding written boundary lines were recorded in the local newspapers. The maps are available at the Family History Library on microfiche and represent most of the larger major cities in the United States such as Chicago, Philadelphia, and New York. www.Ancestry.com has made many of the actual registration cards available online, but for researchers looking up numerous names in one area, these maps are a great asset.

The WWI draft registration cards database can be a useful resource because it covers a significant portion of the U.S. male population in the early twentieth-century. In addition, these cards contain more than just names and dates; they contain significant genealogical information such as birthplace, citizenship status, and information on the individual's nearest relative.

The WWI draft registration cards, 1917–1918 contain a lot of information pertinent to genealogical research. Information that may be found on these cards includes full name, address, age, date of birth, race, citizenship, occupation, employers name, location of employment, name and address of nearest relative, physical description, and signature of registrant, among other things. Use the information to fill in details about your ancestor's life s well as a springboard to lead you to other records. For example, if the address of your ancestor is listed on the draft card, use that information to find your ancestor in a city directory.

The draft cards are also a good source for finding immigrant information because all young men were required to register, regardless of U.S. citizen status, and since 1880–1920 was a high immigration period, a large portion of immigrant men registered and gave information of birth date, birthplace, and in some cases their father's birthplace and nearest relative.

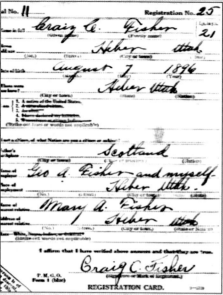

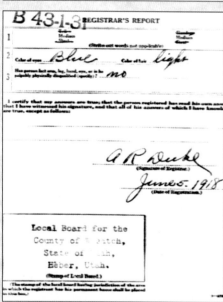

World War 1 Draft Registration for Craig Fisher

Craig Fisher

Craig trained at Fort Douglas in Utah. Just before he was to be shipped out, he was hospitalized for a sudden illness. He missed his shipment date, thus never was deployed. This was comforting to his mother because the women that the men left behind constantly worried for the men's safety.

While the war was still going on, Craig met Mabel Alder at a party in Heber Valley. The community traditionally held a dance whenever any local servicemen came home on leave. These parties also included taffy pulls and candy making events. Craig and Mabel married the May after the war ended when he was discharged from service.

Did you know?

World War I began in 1914 and saw women actively engaged in nursing, driving ambulances, fund raising and Liberty Bond drives, and working in many types of jobs to support the war effort.

World War II

The Japanese attack on Pearl Harbor brought the United States into WWII. The conflict began by most Western accounts on September 3, 1939 due to the German invasion of Poland, and lasted until summer of 1945, involving many of the world's countries. Virtually all countries that participated in World War I were involved in World War II. Many consider World War II to be the only true world war due to the overwhelming number of nations involved and the extraordinary number of theatres—from Europe and the Soviet Union to North Africa, China, South East Asia and the Pacific. In World War I non-European theatres had seen quick and short colonial battles, but in World War II these theatres demanded far more resources and human sacrifice.

This event attributed in varying degrees to the Treaty of Versailles, the Great Depression, and the rise in Nationalism, Fascism, National Socialism, Japanese imperialism, and Militarism.

The war was fought between the Axis Powers, which was formed by the countries Germany, Japan, and Italy, and the Allies. Fighting occurred in Western and Eastern Europe, in the Mediterranean Sea, Africa, the Middle East, in the Pacific and South East Asia, and it continued in China.

About 50 million people died as a result of the war. Few areas of the world were unaffected, the war involved the "home front" and bombing of civilians to a new degree. Atomic weapons, jet aircraft, rockets and radar, the massive use of tanks, submarines, torpedo bombers and destroyer/tanker formations, are only a few of many wartime inventions and new tactics that changed the face of the conflict.

The war sparked a wave of independence for colonies of European powers, who were exhausted from fighting the war. There was a fundamental shift in power from Western Europe to the new superpowers, the United States and the Soviet Union, though there were few actual boundary changes.

"I've found the job where I fit best!"

FIND YOUR WAR JOB
In Industry – Agriculture – Business

Did you know?

For the war effort, women went to work in factories. Women were working to make 20mm, 40mm, 75mm, and 105mm shell casings. The production of these shell casings required for the first time the use of automatic lathes. Rough forgings were hollowed out. Using a lathe, a hole was bored into the nose of each shell, then the nose of each shell was tapped, expanding the hole. Following that the open end of each shell was shaped into a point and both ends were polished. A base was then welded to the face end of each shell before each nearly completed shell casing was turned on a lathe a final time. The shell casings were then subjected to rigorous testing before being heat treated, shipped, and packed.

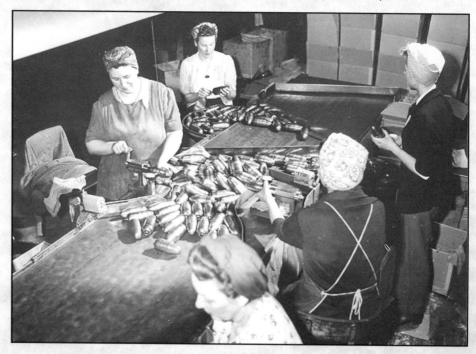

Helene Delattre

In 1939, Helene was 29, and had 4 year old twins. Her husband was a Headmaster in north France. Almost without warning, everything was disorganized. All men left including her husband and her 21 year old brother. All teachers and local authority left. The Germans attacked like lightning. Within a few days, they completed their invasion. They took over all administrative positions, mayoralties, schools, post offices, all mail was stopped. They had plenty of money and bought what they wanted. Shops sold out of essential goods: coffee, flour, butter, and wool.

Then the government declared the end of war for us. France was now under the control of Marshal Petain. Gradually France divided into two rival camps, some for Petain, others for De Gaulle. We feared the bombings by English and American planes that aimed at railways. Many civilians were killed, by miracle none from our family. We waited until after the War ended and the Germans return to their homeland. Afterwards we understood that De Gaulle wasn't a fool, and that Petain delivered France to the Nazis. I do not say that the Americans were wrong to have bombed us. It was necessary to make the Germans submit. My husband always thought that it was by grace of the Americans that twice, in 1914 and in 1939, we were delivered from our enemy.

Did you know?

Women were forced to assume traditional "man" jobs in all fields and were engaged in making the U.S. war industry the most productive manufacturing venture in history. The entrance of women into the workforce changed the entire social and employment structure of the country permanently.

Tip: My great uncle Horace Richardson served in WWI but left no journal. I have found photographs of him but don't know about his experiences. To find out what he may have experienced, I will need to find a journal of someone who served with him. If another soldier was in my uncle's company, he may mention my uncle in his journal.

Rationing

Much of the United States' food is imported from other countries. During WWII it became difficult to bring food into the country by ship, because the German Navy used submarines to bomb any ships. This action put many foodstuffs in short supply. So that everyone would get a fair share of food, the government issued each person a Ration Book. Rationing came into force in January, 1940. Each person could have each week:

- 8p worth of meat
- 3 pints of milk
- 8 ounces of sugar
- 4 ounces of butter or fat
- 4 ounces of bacon
- 2 ounces of tea
- 1 ounce of cheese
- 1 egg

Foods such as rice, jam, biscuits, tinned food and dried fruit were rationed by points. Each family had to register with a shop or store where the food would be bought and this was the only place where the family could shop. Each member of the family had his/her own ration book, adults had a buff colored book, children over three had a blue book and babies had a green book.

Rationed goods included tea, sugar, beef, pork and chocolate.

Many residents which had large backyards converted them into gardens to grow vegetables and henhouses providing a steady stream of fresh eggs.

Others had property holdings large enough to support their own cow and supply themselves with butter, cream, and milk.

Prior to the war people ate large quantities of fried food and meat, drank strong tea, and enjoyed sweet foods such as cake and biscuits. The government feared that rationing would result in a deterioration of health on the homefront but, in fact, the outcome was positive. Rationing resulted in a decline in diet related problems like obesity, diabetes, and heart disease.

Fish, sausages, chicken, ham, and rabbits were not rationed. A "rabbit-o" walked the streets selling rabbits and skinning them for customers on the spot.

A fish monger came to the back door once a week and would scale and fillet fish right then and there.

Did you know?

People developed a number of ways to cope with rationing and make their food supply workable.

- Recipes designed to cater for the lack of eggs, butter, and meat appeared in newspapers and magazines on a regular basis.

- Animal parts such as brains, livers, and kidneys were more readily available than better cuts of meat and formed a significant part of people's diets.

- Hand mincers were popular kitchen appliances at this time. A favorite meal was shepherd's pie made by mincing left over meat and combining the mince with stale bread and eggs.

- Coca Cola, hamburgers, tinned spaghetti, and Spam became common food staples.

- Supermarket shopping became the new way of life.

Tip:
If you have no photographs of your family involved in an historic event that you want to scrapbook, there is plenty of memorabilia online and at the library about the a variety of historic events. When journaling, personalize the situation by relaying how it effected your family.

Christian Flygare

My great grandfather Christian was a well to do businessman. He was the County Commissioner for Ogden City and on numerous boards. When rationing took effect, he converted a portion of his backyard to chicken coops. He taught his children to care for the chickens and collect the eggs. Being one of the rationed items, eggs were a highly sought after product. Christian had his children deliver the eggs daily to the neighbors, especially those with large families who were struggling with their rationing allotment. This story certainly makes sense when Christian in the photograph below is dressed in his business suit standing in the middle of a grouping of chickens.

Tip:
I found the photograph to the left and the story about Christian Flygare after I had already done the above generic page about rationing. I can now incorporate this family story into the above scrapbook pages further personalizing the event and the effect of rationing.

Freedoms

There are numerous people who have spent their lives or sacrificed their lives fighting for freedom. Some were quiet, some are more celebrated. How was your family involved? How are you respecting their work?

Freedom to Worship

Church records began much earlier than civil registration records and in most cases they are the best source to use when there are no civil records. Looking through church records may lead you to find their conversion and if they moved with their congregation to protect their freedom to worship as they chose.

These records can be used to verify other secondary sources such as newspaper articles, obituaries, tombstone and monument inscriptions, and other sources. Religious institutions published materials about their members. Weekly bulletins may still exist somewhere in the community where the church was located, either in a library's special collections area, or in the historical holdings of the church, or its successor church. These may provide information about your ancestor's involvement or may point to joint activities with other churches. Records of dissolved church congregations may have been given to other churches.

Churches often published commemorative histories that listed the names of members, church officers, and clergy over the history of the church. These commemorative volumes are usually issued on key anniversaries of a church's founding or on the occasion of the opening of a new facility.

Contact the church, the local public library, and the local genealogical and historical societies. Also check used bookstores in the community where the church was located.

City directories from the period when your ancestor lived in a community may list which churches of each denomination existed at the time. In the case of a disappeared church, a city directory can help you identify possible other congregations that may have acquired their members and records.

If you do not know the denomination, find the obituary. If the name of the clergy member(s) who officiated at a funeral or memorial service might be included in the obituary, you can often use a city directory to locate the name of that person. There is usually an occupation listed in the older directories, such as "Pastor, 1st Baptist Church." Since there is usually some affiliation, either for the deceased, the spouse, or the grown children, start checking the membership records there. In addition, ask whether the clergy person maintained a diary or journal of ceremonies over which he or she presided; there may be valuable clues in the notes.

Local librarians may know the history of churches in the area, and even members' names, or they may know of a contact in the community who might be of help to you. The library may also have copies of church histories, microfilmed newspapers and other local publications, and correspondence of historical interest in their files. Academic libraries' special collection in the area should be contacted and checked as well, as they too may possess materials that may otherwise have been lost.

State archives are involved in the preservation of materials, relating to communities and their churches, schools, cemeteries, and other facilities. Some have identified every newspaper and periodical published in their state, including religious publications, and have attempted to acquire copies of every issue possible. These have then been microfilmed or scanned, and samples may be accessible on their websites.

When some churches dissolve or merge with others, the records of the original church are sent to a higher administrative office or organization.

Researching Church Records

To find a family's religion search:
- Baptism/confirmation certificates
- Bible records
- Biography
- Cemeteries
- Church records
- Genealogies

My Prayer

My brother Robert and I were taught as children to kneel and say our prayers every night. We were taught to give thanks for our freedom. We were told that it was a privilege to pray in public or in private whenever we chose.

As a 3 year old, I did not know what a "privilege" was. But over the years I have come to learn, understand, and be ever indebted to the many relatives direct or distant that have fought for and protected my right to pray, worship, and practice my religious beliefs. Some have given up their homelands, homes, possessions and in some causes family members to fight for and honor the right to worship. I owe it to them to use this right respectively.

Did you know?

In 1954, Congress created a Prayer Room in the nation's capitol on the west side of the Rotunda. It contains an alter and an open Bible. In this room is a stained glass window picturing George Washington in prayer along with the words of Psalm 16:1. Each business day Congress begins with prayers led by the Senate Chaplain and the House Chaplain.

Declaration of Independence

How did the signing of the document effect your family? To get this far back into history you would either need to be related to someone of importance such as one of the signers that would be documented or find an invaluable journal from an ancestors recording their involvement. Most likely for events in the 1800s you will need to rely on the words of others. First determine where your family was living at the time. Learn as much information about them as you can. Why did they come to America? How involved in freedom were they? Did they participate in founding a community? Sign any public documents? Hold any office? If they were a signer of the Declaration of Independence, how did that effect the rest of their life experience and how did it effect their family?

Did you know?

Benjamin Franklin is quoted as saying: "The Constitution gives people the right to pursue happiness...you have to catch it yourself."

William Walton

William Walton was my 7th great grandfather. When he was 35 years old he signed the Declaration of Independence. The delegates signed in geographical order of states from north to south. George being from Georgia was the last to sign on August 2—the same day that John Hancock signed. William was the only southern delegate who was not a plantation aristocrat. In the eyes of King George, the Declaration was an act of treason. The signers were traitors to the mother country. The punishment could be death by hanging. George knew the consequences but felt strongly about the Declaration. The British soldiers began punishing the signers. They took away their valuables, burned their homes, locked them in prisons. William was not injured by the British soldiers. He went on to become:

- Governor of Georgia, 1779
- Chief Justice, 1783–89
- Presidential Elector and Governor of Georgia, 1789
- Superior Court Judge, 1789–98
- U.S. Senator, 1795

Freedom of Liberty

In 1924, the U.S. Congress voted to make the Pledge of Allegiance the official salute to the flag.

In 1954, on the pledge's 50th birthday one congressman suggested adding two important words to the pledge—"under God." He reminded everyone how Abraham Lincoln called the United States "one nation under God" in his most famous speech. Congress voted to make the change, and President Dwight Eisenhower agreed. He said, "In this way we are declaring the importance of religious faith in America's heritage and future." By repeatedly remembering America's dependence on God's help and protection, President Eisenhower believed "we shall constantly strengthen those spiritual weapons which forever will be our country's most powerful resource in peace and war." Today, pledge proponents think dropping "under God" would rewrite history or threaten religion's legitimate status. Opponents argue the phrase violates church-state separation.

Did you know?

Red Skelton was quoted as saying: "Since I was a small boy, two states have been added to our country, and two words have been added to the Pledge of Allegiance—"under God." Wouldn't it be a pity if someone said, 'That is a prayer,' and that should be eliminated from schools, too?"

Freedom to Protect

Often referred to as the right of self-defense, this freedom assures each citizen that he can lawfully stand up to protect his own, even if the government, which has a fundamental responsibility to protect its citizens, fails in this vital role.

The law permits a person to defend himself, family, loved ones, friends, or even complete strangers.

One may justifiably intervene in defense of any person who is in actual or apparent imminent danger of death or serious bodily harm, and in so doing he may use such force as he has reason to believe, and does believe, necessary under the circumstances. The defender must be reasonable in his belief that the third party is in dire peril of death or serious bodily harm. The defender must also have a reasonable basis to believe that the force he uses is necessary to protect the apparent victim from the threatened harm.

As the western communities grew, it was increasing important to protect your land and family. To homesteaders and new settlers, it was a matter of survival against horse thieves, poachers, Native Americans, and traveling bandits. Many settlers took it upon themselves to protect themselves and neighbors in various situations until actual law enforcement measures were introduced.

Vigilante

Ed Hennessey was a hard working homesteader, who owned a large herd of cattle and a number of acres of land in Arizona. Like many homesteaders, Ed had to stay alert and prepared to protect his land and property.

In the 1920s, whenever the local sheriff or his men could not catch a rustler in the Kingman Arizona area, they would chase him over the Navajo County line and Ed would take care of them. Ed's philosophy was ". . . anyone riding across a cattle man's range with a running iron was assumed guilty and should be hanged."

The sheriff claimed that Ed started catching so many rustlers they had to pin a deputy badge on him to make his work legal.

Interestingly enough, Ed's son George Thomas after his retirement became a guard at the Arizona State Prison. His father had taught him that it was a freedom to protect yourself and the need for consequences for those who abuse others or others' possessions.

George was an effective prison guard. On one occasion when the prisoners were rioting, George drew a gun on an escaping prisoner who had his partner at gunpoint. George would not be threatened and instead of retreating he shot the prisoner in the leg forcing the prisoner to let his partner free. This ended the riot without further bloodshed.

The Regulators

In 1771, South Carolina was under the jurisdiction of the Council in Charleston, but little help was offered to the back country. Subsequently because there were no law enforcement, courts, or jails to protect the inhabitants from wandering ruffians and bullies, the settlers of the area organized "the Regulators." While the men were away, the bullies came on their land and took whatever they wanted including horses, wagons, and cattle and harassed their wives.

Among the 19 men that made up the regulators my great grandfather Robert Stark possessed at least 1000 acres of land. He joined with the other regulators to protect their property by catching, punishing, and getting rid of the troublemakers. Though the men were arrested in the name of the King for acting out of authority, Robert Stark was eventually named Sheriff by the Governor and ordered to build a courthouse and a jail.

Tip:
If you can't find your own relative in an event, read the journals of his neighbors or those doing the same job as he did to get an idea of what life was like and how your relative fit into society. If you know his religion, occupation, when and where he lived, then with some research you can make a generalization about his life.

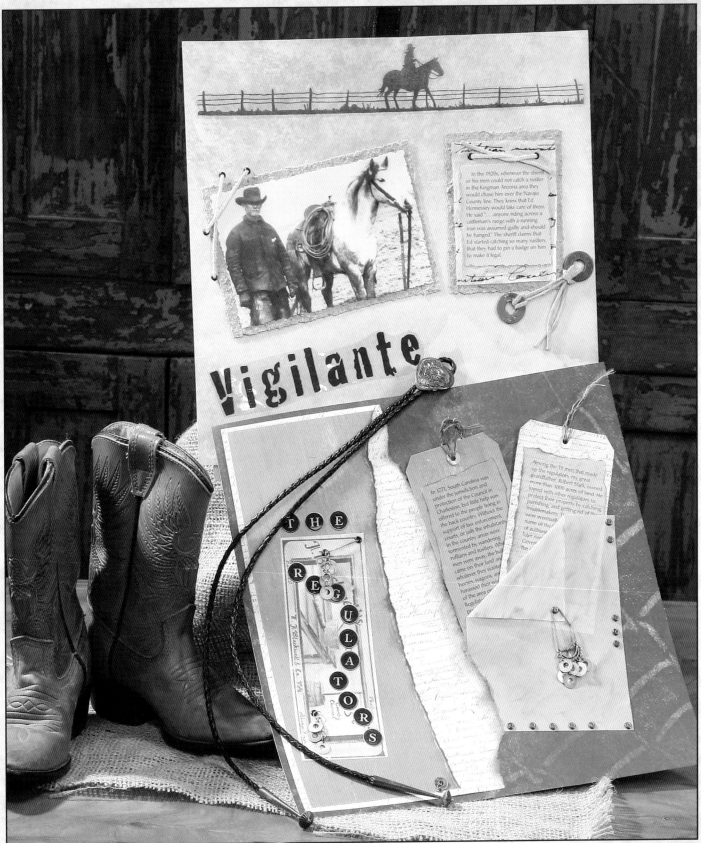

Prohibition

In 1919, Prohibition became nationwide when the 18th Amendment was added to the Constitution. The leaders of the prohibition movement were alarmed at the drinking behavior of Americans and new immigrants. Because liquor was not legally available during the 1920s, the public turned to gangsters who readily took on the bootlegging industry and supplied them with liquor. On account of the industry being so profitable, more gangsters became involved in the money-making business. Gangsters such as Al Capone consolidated the illegal liquor trade on many of the same principles used to consolidate the automobile and steel industries. As a result of the money involved in the bootlegging industry, there was much rival between gangs. The profit motive resulted in over 400 gang related murders a year in Chicago alone. Although the consumption of liquor dropped substantially during the prohibition, illegal drinking by millions created an illegitimate billion-dollar industry. Prohibition was repealed in 1933.

Slavery

There is no such thing as a "slave record". Legal records in the 19th century were about the personal rights and property rights of free persons, and slaves had no personal or property rights. Slaves do not appear as parties to any lawsuit, marriage, contract, deed, bond, or court action. They did not make wills or inherit property. They are not named in the tax digests. They do not appear on any jury list, land lottery, school roster, or voters list. And yet, tens or hundreds of thousands of individual slaves are named and described in the court records, their lives inseparably intermingled with the lives of free citizens with whom they lived.

One of the greatest challenges in tracing slave ancestors is to trace individual slaves back through former owners, because the identifying owners' names usually changes without a clue. A slave typically appears in the records of an owner's legal affairs with no indication of where he came from. Records of sale or transfer are essential to trace individual slaves from owner to owner.

One of the biggest genealogical challenges is to connect a person's free identity with his or her former slave identity. When all other evidence is lacking, we are sometimes forced to speculate by matching freed persons' last names with the last names of slave owners.

Pre-1865 legal records to review for slave data

- Because slaves were property, they may be found in any record which documents property rights.

- Because slaves were accountable under the law for criminal acts, they were present in criminal court records as defendants and witnesses, but even more slaves are identified in the criminal records of white persons who traded illegally with slaves, stole slaves, or had other improper relations with slaves.

- A slave's legal identity was the combination of his first name and the full name of his owner. It is essential whenever extracting slave data about slaves that their owners' full names, as given in the record, also be extracted.

- Check Homestead applications if you feel your ancestor received land. As part of the request, the applicant names his spouse and children. Petitions also list all personal property and real estate owned by the petitioner.

- Deeds and mortgages of slaves document part of the people belonging to certain slavemasters during the masters' lifetime. Mortgage records can be the only source for the identities of some slaves who were later emancipated by the Civil War. Slave mortgages name persons and identify family kinship.

- Conditional sales of slaves were extremely common. Usually the last resort of a slaveowner deep in debt, the conditional sale was like pawning his property. Title to the property, and possessions, went to a major creditor, but the seller held the right to repurchase his property for a prescribed amount, within a prescribed time.

- Prenuptial agreements were often executed between wealthy widows who were about to remarry, and their prospective husbands. These contracts were designed to protect the woman's property from being squandered by the man. They commonly include slave information.

- In civil suits, details about the lives of particular slaves and their families, the relationships between master and slave, and working and living conditions. The tangled transfers of ownership experienced by some slaves are explained here, as well as the growth and break-up of some slave families.

- All criminal trials should be read for slave content. Whites were tried for crimes like selling liquor to slaves, unauthorized trading with slaves, receiving stolen goods from slaves, playing cards with Negroes, harboring runaways, Sabbath-breaking (making slaves work on Sunday), stealing or assaulting slaves, committing adultery and fornication with slaves, and other crimes.

- Divorce papers usually list owned property to help the court decide alimony issues.

Underground Railroad

This secret abolitionist organization, which had hiding places, or stations, throughout the Northern states and even into Canada, brought enslaved people out of the south. Moving at night, agents of the Underground Railroad followed the North Star to guide them as they led slaves to freedom.

From 1786 to 1865 fugitive slaves escaped to northern states and Canada, some 50,000 slaves in all. If your ancestors settled in a northern city, Canada or a city in the Midwest before the end of the Civil War, chances are they traveled on the Underground Railroad.

Much of our cultural and religious heritage derived from our ethnic roots. While each ethnic group faces different research challenges within United States records, most use the same basic resources to conduct research. There are however, unique challenges for the African-American researcher. Because of the special nature of African American experiences in the United States, research takes a different turn very quickly from other ethnic groups.

African Americans use the same records: vital, military, census. There is however a difference in using these records. As African Americans were segregated in every aspect of their lives so were their records. Birth, death, and marriage records were often segregated in city, county, and state repositories. Listings in city directories were segregated by white and colored listing, often placing African Americans in the back of the book. Cemeteries and cemetery records were segregated. Varying from state to state, vital records may also be separated by race. Over the years, the records have been confused as to the color so check both the white and black records. Listings of African American records were routinely omitted from compiled records and indexes. If you don't find what you are looking for in compiled records find the original document.

Reconstruction was a time to repair the damage done during the Civil War and a time for assisting former slaves in making the transition from slavery to freedom. Established in 1865, the Freedman Bureau established schools to teach former slaves to read and write, passed out food and medical supplies to refugees of the Civil War, managed property abandoned and confiscated from former Confederates, established hospitals, conducted trials for acts of violence, supervised labor contracts between former slaves and former slave owners, monitored apprenticeship contracts and legalized marriages during slavery. Each one of these polices created records that were preserved by the federal government and are available for research at the National Archives.

During the same time, a banking system for former slaves and veterans of the Civil War was established. The Freedman's Savings and Trust Company's records are rich resources of genealogical material. These records can be found at the National Archives. They list places of residence and birth, other family member names, sometimes names of former slave owners and Civil War regiments.

There were African Americans who fought on both sides of the Civil War. The National Archives have records for these African American participants.

By the time you reach 1865 in your research, you should have determined whether your ancestors were slaves or not. Do not assume they were slaves and skip directly to slave research. It is a false assumption that all African Americans are descended from slaves.

Researching African American Records

Afro-American Historical and Genealogical Society
P.O. Box 73086
Washington, DC 20056-3086

African-American Family History Association
P.O. Box 115268
Atlanta, GA 30310

There are five distinct periods of the African-American experience that should be considered when researching African-American genealogical:
- Civil Rights Movement 1954-1970
- Segregation 1896-1954
- Reconstruction 1865-1877
- Civil War 1861-1865
- Slavery 1526-1865

Since slaves could not read, they taught one another coded songs about the North Star. The slaves hoped to escape to a safe house. The movement from one safe house to another was referred to as the Underground Railroad. The slaves continued northward by following the Big Dipper which they referred to as the "drinking gourd."

Harriet Tubman with slaves she saved using the Underground Railroad

Journey

Drinking gourd

North Star

Underground Railroad

Excursion

AM I NOT A MAN AND A BROTHER

TO BE SOLD, on board the Ship *Bance Island*, on tuesday the 6th of May next, at *Ashley Ferry*; a choice cargo of 250 fine healthy NEGROES, just arrived from the Windward & Rice Coast.—The utmost care has already been taken, and shall be continued, to keep them free from the least danger of being infected with the SMALL-POX, no boat having been on board, and all other communication with people from *Charles-Town* prevented.
Austin, Laurens, & Appleby.

discover

adventure

Slaves—five generations

uncharted territory

Women's Rights

During World War I, women took jobs in factories to support the war. After the war, the National American Woman Suffrage Association reminded the President and Congress that women's war work should be rewarded with recognition of their political equality. President Wilson responded by beginning to support the woman's suffrage movement. In a speech on September 18, 1918, he said, "We have made partners of the women in this war. Shall we admit them only to a partnership of suffering and sacrifice and toil and not to a partnership of right?"

Less than a year later, the House of Representatives proposed an Amendment to the Constitution.

On August 26, 1920, the 19th Amendment to the United States Constitution became law, and women could vote in the fall elections, including the Presidential election.

Did you know?

In the early 20th century, makeup just came into acceptability. When the suffragettes wore lipstick during their campaigns they sent the message that it was acceptable to wear make-up.

Amelia Flygare

My great grandmother Millie was active in the democratic party. She was Chairman of the Weber County Women's Organization and one of the founders of the Girl Scouts program in her area. Her name appeared in her local newspaper repeatedly for numerous projects she was working with in the community.

Her husband was the county commissioner and her four sons served honorably in WWI. I don't know the details of her contribution, but knowing her involvement in politics and the women's movement, I would assume Millie was heavily involved in obtaining the right to vote for women. This is a subject I get to research until I know all the facts. I dedicated this page to her and will add more facts to the page as I find them.

Tragedies

A wide variety of tragedies have happened throughout the generations. Some are natural disasters, some are man caused, others are unexplained. Regardless, they affect families. These situations tend to show the true character of the people involved by how they reacted, recovered and coped.

Bermuda Triangle

The Bermuda Triangle is an area located off the southeastern Atlantic coast of the United States, which is noted for a high incidence of unexplained losses of ships, boats, and aircraft. Over 1500 people have vanished in the Bermuda Triangle over the past 50 years.

The heart of the triangle lies between Florida, Bermuda, and Puerto Rico. Countless theories attempting to explain the disappearances have been offered. The most practical seem to be environmental and those citing human error. The majority of disappearances can be attributed to the area's unique environmental features. The area is one of the two places on earth that a magnetic compass does not point towards true north. The amount of variation changes by as much as 20 degrees as one circumnavigates the earth. If this compass variation or error is not compensated for, a navigator could find himself far off course and in deep trouble.

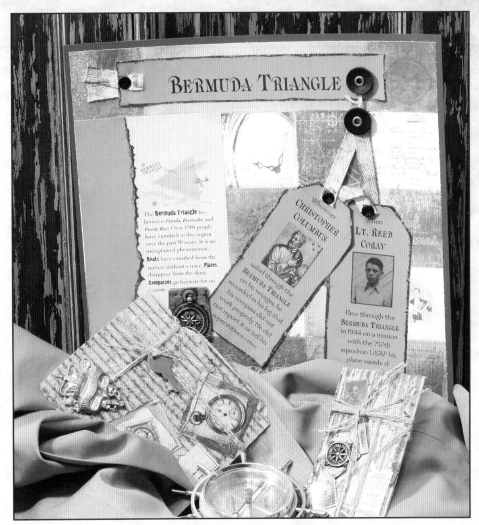

Reed Coray

My great cousin Lt. Coray was with the 757th squadron USAF. In 1944, he was missing in action over the Bermuda Triangle. Never to be heard from again. My grandmother knew when she hugged him goodbye he would not return from the war. In a dream after the funeral, she saw his plane burst into flames over the ocean and only remnants fell into the ocean. She then knew what had happened.

Tip:
Whenever a relative goes to war and you cannot find him again find out if he returned from the war or not. If not find out why? Check his military records for any missing in action or other information. Read in journals of family members during the time he was away for any reports of his activities. Look at his tombstone for any markings indicating where and why he died.

Witch Trials

Reading was a popular pastime during the winter months in the Puritan settlement of Salem Massachusetts. There was an interest in books about prophecy and fortune telling throughout New England during the winter of 1691-1692. These books were especially popular among young girls and adolescents. Girls formed small, informal circles to practice the fortune telling they learned from their reading.

Betty Parris, her cousin Abigail Williams, and two other friends formed such a circle. Tituba, Rev. Parris' slave whom he bought while on a trip to Barbados, would often participate in the circle. She would entertain the others with stories of witchcraft, demons, and mystic animals. Other girls soon joined the circle to listen to Tituba's tales and participate in the fortune telling experiments.

Puritans believed in witches and their ability to harm others. They defined witchcraft as entering into a pact with the devil in exchange for certain powers to do evil. Thus, witchcraft was considered a sin because it denied God's superiority, and a crime because the witch could call up the devil in his shape to perform cruel acts against others. Therefore, when witchcraft was suspected, it was important to investigate the claim thoroughly and the tormentor(s) identified and judged.

The girls continued to learned tricks and spells and found that the more dramatic they acted the more attention they got, thus the less bored they were. Their behavior turned into a scandal. The adults believed the girls were possessed. A doctor examined the girls and concluded that "the evil hand was on them." The people, scared that the devil was in Salem, demanded that the girls divulge the names of the evil spirits. The girls began randomly naming village people that they did not like.

They named three women who were prime candidates for the accusations of witchcraft. Sarah Osborne was an elderly lady who had not gone to church in over a year, and poor church attendance was a Puritan sin.

Sarah Good was a homeless woman who begged door to door. If people failed to give her alms, she would utter unknown words and leave. Residents would often attribute her visits to death of livestock. They believed the mumbled words she spoke under her breath were curses against them.

They also accused the slave Tituba. The accused villagers were brought into court. Though they all pled innocent, the girls continued to act possessed. Two magistrates from Salem Town, John Hathorne and Jonathan Corwin traveled to Salem to investigate the cases.

During the questioning of the three accused, Betty, Abigail, and six other girls would often scream and tumble on the floor of the meetinghouse. Even with the harsh questioning by the two magistrates and the unusual actions of the afflicted girls, Sarah Good and Sarah Osborne maintained their innocence. Tituba, however, confessed for three days.

During Tituba's confession, she stated that a man clothed in black made her sign in a book, and that Sarah Good, Sarah Osborne, and others, whose names she could not read, had also signed this book.

Any negative event now was interpreted by the Puritans as the cause of God's wrath. Due to this belief and fear, they wanted to be certain that every last witch was discovered and punished in order to end His anger. By the end of May in 1692, about 200 people were jailed under the charges of witchcraft.

Among others Rebecca Nurse was accused. This 71-year-old woman did not make for a likely witch. She was kind, generous and well liked by the community. She was the only one of the accused who escaped a guilty verdict. However, when the jurors announced a not guilty verdict in her case, the afflicted girls howled, thrashed about, and rolled around on the floor. With the courtroom in an uproar, the judges asked the jury to reconsider its decision. When they did, a guilty verdict was returned. Rebecca Nurse, along with the other four convicted women, were hanged July 19, 1692 on Gallows Hill. Eventually 20 of the wrongly accused town folk were hung.

Fourteen years later, one of the girls admitted to the town that they had lied and made the story up.

Rebecca Nurse was one of the towns people accused of being a witch.

Rebecca was taken from her sick bed to testify in court. During her testimony, one of the accusing girls fell into convulsions and then another and then all the girls together. In response to their behavior, Rebecca replied "Oh Lord, help me!" and spread her hands helplessly. Her very gesture became an accusation against her, for the girls immediately spread their arms and copied every movement Rebecca made. Every spectator believed Rebecca was guilty, saying "words may lie, but deeds could not." In front of those in the courtroom Rebecca was demonstrating witchcraft.

Though Rebecca's family defended her the best they could, she was hanged with four others towns people on 19 July 1692 on Gallows Hill.

Author Nathaniel Hawthorne

REBECCA NURSE
HANGED
JULY 19, 1692

Norman Younker

Having majored in history with an emphasis in early American history, Norman was excited to discover that his fourth great grandmother was tried and convicted in Salem, Massachusetts of being a witch. He and his children are honored to have descended from such a great and noble person. "Rebecca Nurse's example of patience and forgiveness during the persecutions, imprisonment, and trial that preceded her death (she was hung) has humbled and inspired us. We are grateful to know we are a part of her family."

Did you know?

Author Nathaniel Hawthorne was a descendant of Judge John Hathorne, one of the justices at the Salem witch trials. When Hawthorne learned of their relationship, he changed his last name to disassociate himself from the behavior of his ancestor.

Stockmarket Crash

In late October 1929 investors in New York City began to panic. Stocks that they had bought at high prices began to drop in value. More and more investors sold their stocks at whatever price they could get. Over two days, the value of companies being traded on the stock exchange fell almost 13 percent on Monday and another 12 percent the next day. Fortunes were wiped out. The stock market crashed. This is the most famous crash in U.S. history. A common story of those effected included a wealthy high rollers on Wall Street resorting to selling apples out of a box for a nickel. Eventually he like many jumped out of a building.

The 1929 crash was spectacular by any measure. It followed a spectacular bull market that had been going on for the better part of a decade. The Dow Industrials hit a high of 386 in September, 1929. It did not get back to that level until November, 1954. At its worst level, the Dow dropped to 40.56 in July, 1932. That is a drop of 89%.

Tip:

Some photographs may bring about recollections of certain historical periods. The wedding picture taken of your grandparents in 1933 may provoke you to learn about their marriage ceremony, and about their experiences during the stockmarket crash. If your grandparents are no longer around to share their stories, use the numerous resources on the Internet and in the library, to illuminate this time period.

Depression

A prolonged slump in agriculture, industrial overproduction, high tariffs, and the stock market crash in 1929 all contributed to the worst economic depression in the nation's history. By 1932, millions of Americans were out of work. The amount of goods and services produced by American companies plunged. People all over the country stood in lines to get bread or eat at free soup kitchens. The US did not recover for 12 years.

Depression Problems

- Fear of losing jobs and unemployment cause anxiety
- People became depressed and attempted suicide
- Thousands went hungry
- Children suffered long term effects from a poor diet and inadequate medical care
- Living conditions changed when multiple families crowded into small houses or apartments
- Divorces decreased because couples could not afford separate households while others postponed wedding plans
- Unemployed men felt like failures when they could not support their families and lost their status when they saw their wives and children working to the point where they were too ashamed to get relief or help from friends
- Women were blamed for taking the jobs of men
- Women continued to work, yet were paid less than men

OUT OF WORK

With the effects of the Depression, Ralph Flygare found himself without work to support his family. He sold his expensive home in California and moved to a small farm in Star Valley, Wyoming. His children grew up in Star Valley always wishing to return to the "good life" they enjoyed in California, but the family never recovered financially.

FREE SOUP COFFEE & DOUGHNUTS FOR THE UNEMPLOYED

SOUP KITCHEN

In 1930, people lined up at soup kitchens, operated by gangster Al Capone. The government made few efforts to help citizens fight the effects of the Depression.

MONOPOLY

The game in which each player's goal is to make money while forcing the opponents into bankruptcy, originated and flourished, oddly enough, during the height of the Great Depression.

Did you know?

Al Capone, America's best known gangster, shocked Chicago in 1930 by setting up Chicago's first free soup kitchen for people who had been thrown out of work by the deepening Depression. Preceding the passage of the Social Security Act, "soup kitchens" provided the only meals some unemployed Americans had. Some believed Capone embarked on this campaign to restore his image and to win public favor that had turned against him, a publicity stunt, by helping the average working man; but others argue that Capone became a folk hero, providing as many as 3,000 meals daily, ordering merchants to give clothes and food to the needy at his expense, paying for heating and giving money to the poor.

Illness

In the fall of 1918, WWI was winding down and peace was on the horizon. An estimated 675,000 Americans died of influenza during the pandemic, ten times as many as in the world war. The influenza pandemic circled the globe.

The pandemic affected everyone. Even President Woodrow Wilson suffered from the flu in early 1919 while negotiating the treaty of Versailles to end the World War. Those who were able to avoid infection had to deal with the public health ordinances to restrain the spread of the disease. The public health departments distributed gauze masks to be worn in public. Stores could not hold sales and funerals were limited to 15 minutes. A signed certificate was necessary to enter some towns and ride railroads. Besides the lack of health care workers and medical supplies, there was a shortage of coffins, morticians, and gravediggers.

Diseases and physical ailments were potentially catastrophic in other eras. Before the introduction of antibiotics, and vaccines, our forebears suffered a wide variety of illnesses. Typhoid fever, mumps, measles, chicken pox, cancer, tuberculosis, heart disease, influenza, kidney failure, dysentery, bone fractures, pneumonia, and so many other illnesses for which we have treatments and cures today terminated the lives of our ancestors far too soon.

Research Family Illness

To determine the health of your family members review:

- medical records
- letters and diaries
- cemetery caretaker records

Be diligent in keeping a health record of yourself and your family members. This will not only assist you in further health issues and questions you may need information for, but your descendants may be helped by this information in diagnosing their own health situation and solutions.

Diseases were commonly cited in historic obituaries and death certificates. Listed below are the historic name and what it would be called today:

Historic Disease	Modern Description
Ablepsy	Blindness
Ague	Malarial Fever
American plague	Yellow fever
Apoplexy	Paralysis due to stroke
Bad Blood	Syphilis
Bilious fever	Typhoid, malaria
Biliousness	Liver disease
Black plague	Bubonic plague
Bladder in throat	Diphtheria
Brain fever	Meningitis
Bronze John	Yellow fever
Bule	Boil, tumor or swelling
Cachexy	Malnutrition
Cacospysy	Irregular pulse
Catalepsy	Seizures/trances
Chin cough	Whopping cough
Chlorosis	Iron deficiency anemia
Cholera	Severe contagious diarrhea
Cholelithiasis	Gall stones
Consumption	Tuberculosis
Corruption	Infection
Cramp colic	Appendicitis
Croup	Diphtheria, strepthroat
Cynanche	Diseases of throat
Dropsy	Swelling caused by kidney/heart disease
Elephantiasis	A form of leprosy
Enteric fever	Typhoid fever
Falling sickness	Epilepsy
French pox	Syphilis
Glandular fever	Mononucleosis
Green fever	Anemia
Grippe/grip	Influenza

Grocer's itch	Skin disease caused by mites in sugar/flour
Heart sickness	Loss of body salt
Hemiplegy	Paralysis of one side of body
Hydrocephalus	Water on the brain
Hydrophobia	Rabies
Hypertrophic	Enlargement of an organ
Infantile paralysis	Polio
Jail fever	Typhus
King's evil	Tuberculosis of neck
Kruchhusten	Whopping cough
Lagrippe	Influenza
Long sickness	Tuberculosis
Lues disease	Syphilis
Lues venera	Venereal disease
Lumbago	Back pain
Lung fever	Pneumonia
Lung sickness	Tuberculosis
Marasmus	Malnutrition
Mortification	Gangrene
Nephrosis	Kidney degeneration
Nostalgia	Homesickness
Paroxysm	Convulsion
Phthiriasis	Lice infestation
Pleurisy	Pain in the chest area
Podagra	Gout
Putrid fever	Diphtheria
Quinsy	Tonsillitis
Remitting fever	Malaria
Rickets	Disease of skeletal system
Sciatica	Rheumatism in hips
Scirrhus	Cancerous tumors
Septicemia	Blood poisoning
Shingles	Viral disease
Strangery	Rupture
Thrush	Spots on mouth, lips and throat

Hennessey Children

Lillie, the mother of the Hennessey children lost her baby to croup. After that incident, she was overly cautious with her other children whenever they seemed ill.

Her son George had a tendency to have spells of the croup. With each attack, Lillie would have his sister Leola hold his nose shut and feed him castor oil. Then Lillie would get a spoon of sugar and put a few drops of kerosene on it to cut the flem in his throat.

On one occasion, George was badly burned when he fell into a wash pot where his mother was boiling corn and lye water to make hominy. The children were expected to stir the mixture but George was much too small to reach. George fell in and scalded his hands and arms. Lillie grabbed him and applied White Feather (Karo syrup) and bandaged them loosely. George healed fine without even a scar.

At one point her children were quarantined due to an illness and sent to stay with her father-in-law. Lillie continued to sneak treats into her children, risking becoming ill herself.

Did you know?

Early midwesterners resorted to their own remedies such as:

- charms
- potions
- home remedies
- a bag of live insects hung around the victims neck

Did you know?

In case you have admired a so-called "sleeping porch" on an old house, you would probably be surprised to learn that this architectural feature was developed specifically for patients with consumption which today is called tuberculous.

Reba
Kennington Miller
was killed at the age of
24 when she was struck by
lightening during a
thunderstorm. The lightening
bolt came
through a
window into
the kitchen
where Reba
was visiting
with her brother
and sister-in-law in
Thayne, Wyoming.
She left behind
two daughters
ages 3 and 4.
Her husband
Frank Miller
remarried
and raised
the girls.
8 Aug 1941

Struck by Lightening

Years ago death by lightening was more common than one would think. The homes were built with metal chimneys and stove pipes which directed a lightening strike directly into the busiest room in the home—the kitchen.

Reba Miller

Reba was watching a rainstorm from the kitchen window when lightening struck the nearby stove pipe. Lightening hit the house and came down the stove pipe. The electric shock killed her instantly. Reba left a husband and two small daughters who never got to know their mother. The event was not uncommon and some have been know to have been struck through the windows of their house while they were sitting on a chair or sofa.

Did you know?

If lightening strikes the phone line outside the house, the strike will travel to every phone on the line—and potentially to anyone holding the phone.

Lightening has the ability to strike a house or near a house and impart an electrical charge to the metal pipes used for plumbing. This puts anyone near the bath tub or shower at risk. The threat today is not as great because PVC is used for indoor plumbing.

Did you know?

Any contact with metal in a lightening storm may prove to be fatal. Two women were killed by a bolt of lightning in London's Hyde Park when their underwired bras acted as conductors.

Mount St. Helens

On May 18, 1980 a magnitude 5.1 earthquake shook Mount St. Helens in Washington state. Fifty seven people were killed and hundreds of miles of land were damaged or destroyed.

When Mount St. Helens erupted, the top 1,300 feet disappeared within minutes. The blast area covered an area of more than 150 square miles and sent thousands of tons of ash into the upper atmosphere.

The blast was a wake-up call to the scientific community and the emergency management community, and the society at large. It reminded people that the Cascade volcanoes are an active volcanic range and the same process that formed the peaks seen today can change during their lifetime in the matter of minutes.

Jill Hennessey

Jill was sitting in her dining room with her family in Spokane, Washington when Mt. St. Helen's erupted. It was a bright sunny day. "We noticed it was getting increasingly darker sooner than normal for the afternoon. My children and I went out on the back porch and saw the sky was a huge gray cover with only an edge of blue sky showing at the skyline. We turned on the television to learn of the phenomenon. My children were scared not knowing what to expect."

To find possible natural disasters which may have happened to your ancestors, refer to one or more of the following sources:

- almanacs
- journals
- history books
- local and national newspapers
- personal letters

Tip:
The ash in the above photograph is actual ash from the Mount St. Helen's eruption on 1980. Jill scooped up this ash from her front yard as everything was covered with several inches of ash even though she was 200 miles from the volcano. I preserved some of this ash in protected plastic sleeves and used it in the actual layout above.

Entertainment

The introduction of the the railroad, telegraph, and telephone combined with new forms of corporate organization which increased leisure time. Improved transportation and communication brought traveling circuses and Wild West shows, and professional baseball.

Literature/Games

Though shows, operas, and musicals were more accessible as years went by, the standard games and activities including reading have remained a popular pastime. Especially for children living on ranches or further away from other children.

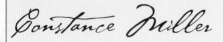

Learning about the passions and enjoyment of ancestors helps you to appreciate things of the past and brings the relative more to life. It took me a while to understand that my grandmother was a child once too and not always a grandmother. When I would go to visit she would read me "Treasure Island." It was later that I learned that this was her favorite book at my age and she was sharing that passion with me. I still chuckle to think that my little granny wanted to be a pirate and sail the open seas.

Popular games from a century ago:

- Draughts (similar to checkers was a favorite game of George Washington)
- Hand Puppets
- Hand Shadows
- Hoop & Stick
- Hide and Go Seek
- Hopscotch
- Horizontal Tops (wooden disc with two strings that pass through two holes drilled on opposite sides of the disc. When the strings are pulled tight, the disc spins; and when the strings are relaxed slightly, the disc rewinds to spin again)
- Jacks
- Jackstraws (this game similar to "Pick-Up Sticks" was introduced to early settlers by the Indians)
- Jacob's Ladder
- Kick the Can
- Marbles
- Red Rover
- Ring Toss
- See-Saw
- Stilts
- Yo-Yo

Bowling Green

The Southampton Old Bowling Green in England is the oldest Green in the world. The Green itself has been cared for since 1187, in the reign of Richard I the Lionheart.

The Bowling game is played by placing a jack or a penny anywhere on the green. Each player takes a turn rolling his two bowls at the jack. When the bowl comes to a rest it is measured and the distance from the jack is recorded before the bowl is removed. After all the players have bowled, the player with the closest bowl is awarded one point. If he also has the second nearest he scores two points. The jack is then placed at a different location and the game continues until someone scores seven points.

The winner is made a knight-of-the-green and can never enter the competition again. It is rare for the knight to be declared on the first day. The competition has been known to last for ten days.

My eighth great grandfather, Samuel Miller, was master of the Old Green in 1776 and founder of the Knighthood Competition which is still played annually.

Crown Green or Lawn Bowling was the leading sport in America before the Revolutionary War. Considered the "Sport of Kings," bowling was played in America by George Washington, John D. Rockefeller, George Vanderbilt, and Walt Disney—who sent planeloads of bowlers to his Palm Springs home for bowling weekends.

Samuel Miller

My eighth great grandfather, Samuel Miller was master of the Old Green in 1776 and founder of the famous Knighthood Competition.

Did you know?

When Sir Francis Drake was informed that the Spanish Armada was near on 18 July 1588 he was playing a game of Bowls on Plymouth Hoe. His reputed response was, " We still have time to finish the game and to thrash the Spaniards too."

Reap the Reward

As you research, historical events will come alive for you and cause you to reflect on your own life and how you have been effected as well as how you are effecting others.

Royalty

When giving advice to new a researcher, I often say "don't just look for kings and queens but the 'royal' people you are actually related to." However, when I found that I was related to both Prince Charles and Princess Diana through different family lines, I must say it is fun to think I was from royal blood.

Princess Diana

Lady Diana Spencer became the Princess of Wales, when she married Prince Charles in 1981. Diana's grandfather claimed that the word Spencer derives from the Norman word for Steward, or Head of Household: Despenser and that their ancestor was steward to the household of William the Conqueror in 1066. From the early 16th century Diana's forebears had moved beyond their origins as sheep farmers to forge intimate connections with the English court. There was an earlier Lady Diana Spencer, who nearly married the Prince of Wales in 1730 and who like the modern Diana, died tragically young.

Princess Diana

Did you know?

Sir Winston Churchill (1874-1965) was of the Spencer family. For generations, his family name was hyphenated as Spencer-Churchill. English on his father's side, American on his mother's, Sir Winston Leonard Spencer Churchill enjoyed a rich historic inheritance. Winston, after the Royalist family with whom the Churchills married before the English Civil War; Leonard, after his grandfather, Leonard Jerome of New York; Spencer, the married name of a daughter of the 1st duke of Marlborough, from whom the family descended; Churchill, the family name of the 1st duke, which his descendants resumed after the Battle of Waterloo. All these strands come together in a career that had no parallel in British history.

124

Carry on

With as much time and effort as you put into your research and preservation, be certain to share your treasure with your family, especially with children. Creating an excitement and desire in others will ensure that the work continues after you have left. Educate others so the works you have so tenderly prepared will not be pushed aside and lost or destroyed but will be cared for and added to as they should be.

Excite others into continuing your work
- Involve grandchildren in making scrapbook pages with you when they come to visit.
- Display family treasures at family reunions and other family gatherings.
- Copy scrapbook pages and give to family members as gifts.
- Tell family stories to children and grandchildren during quiet moments before bed or around holiday times when one feels closer to family.
- Design a page about a daughter or grandchild and include it in the book of ancestors. Remind her that she is just as vital to the family as her ancestors and offers no less than they did in participating in historical events and the family.

Recommended Sources

Genealogical Societies

Federation of Genealogical Societies
P.O. Box 200940
Austin, TX 78720-0940
www.fgs.org

National Genealogical Society Library
4527 17th St., N.
Arlington, VA 22207-2399
www.ngsgenealogy.org

National Society of the Daughters of
the American Revolution
1776 D Street
Washington DC. 20006-5303
www.dar.org/library/library.html

New England Historic
Genealogical Society
101 Newbury St
Boston, MA 02116
www.nehgs.org

The Library of Congress
1st-2nd Streets, NW
Washington, D.C. 20006
www.loc.gov

The National Archives
Pennsylvania Avenue at 8th Street, N.W.
Washington, D.C. 20408
www.nara.gov

The Federation of Genealogical
Societies
PO Box 3385
Salt Lake City, UT 84110

M.R.S. Hobby Shop
www.mrshobby.com

Internet Resources

www.ancestry.com
access to limited number of free
databases. Membership is required
to access numerous commercial
databases.

www.cyndislist.com
contains multiple search indexes
that list thousands of genealogy
links to information and records

www.everton.com
evertons genealogical helper-online
magazine, searchable databases,
resources, references

www.familysearch.org
access to free online database
containing hundreds of millions
of names and resources

www.rootsweb.com
oldest and largest online free
genealogical website.

www.usgenweb.org
volunteers working together to
provide access to websites for
genealogical research

www.vitalrec.com/links.html
contains links to US and international vital records offices, adoption
resources, surname searches.

Bibliography

Bermuda Triangle

Bermuda Triangle
Andrew Donkin
DK Publishing, Inc. 2000

Bob Hope

The Spirit of Bob Hope One
Hundred Years One Million Laughs
by Richard Grudens
Celebrity Profiles Publishing Box
344 Main St Stony Brook, NY 11790

Bowling Green

Ye History offe ye olde
Southampton Bowling Green
by Sir Bert Baker
The Sholing Press, Southampton
England, 1980

Fashions

Pictures from American Victorian
Costume in Early Photographs
by Priscilla Harris Dalrymple
Dover Publications, 1991

Ellis Island

Ellis Island: a New Beginning
by Laura Best 1995

Freedom of Religion

In God We Trust: Stories of Faith
in American History
byTimothy Crater
and Ranelda Hunsicker
Chariot Victor Publishing 1997

Hawthorne Witch Trials

The Salem Witch Trials
by Lori Lee Wilson
Lerner Publications Co. 1997

Longfellow-Mayflower

Proving Your Pedigree
by Archibald F. Bennett
Deseret Sunday School Board
Salt Lake City 1951

Native American Expansion

An American History
by Rebecca Brooks Gruver
Meredith Corporation 1972

Princess Diana

The Spencers: A Personal History
of an English Family
by Charles Spencer
ST. Martin's Press New York 1999

About the Author

Laura Best has authored the highly acclaimed books: *Genealogy for the First Time, Scrapbooking your Family History*, and *Memories of a Lifetime: Family History*. She also shares her passion for family history with the youth through her Belonging to Family series.

Laura Best is a versatile writer, editor, and genealogist. She is a popular lecturer and speaks at numerous writing conferences and genealogy seminars. Laura has been a student of family history all of her life and is the chairman of her family genealogy society comprised of members nationwide as well as throughout England.

Acknowledgements

Special thanks to my husband Lon Elbert and my support team—Jill Hennessey, Christie, Lisa, Katie, and Sara Best, Justin and Stephanie Otting, Jaci Elbert, and Mike Greve.

My appreciation to Jack Cooper; Larry and Mary Gillette; Barbra Harvey; JoAnn Hatch; George Hennessey; Paul Hokanson; and Margaret Ostlund; Norman, Kathy, Tess, Ben, and Misha Younkers who were gracious enough to let me share their family with you.

Index